Managing Risk with Derivatives

A Guide for Bankers and Their Customers

Townsend Walker

AMERICAN BANKERS ASSOCIATION ®

Printed in the United States of America

To

Stormy

Contents

Illustrations *Page*

Tables *Page*

PREFACE

This book is a valuable tool for bankers and their business customers who want to learn how derivatives hedge interest rate exposure. It is also for bankers concerned with asset/liability management. It is a *practical* guide describing how to define and measure interest rate exposure, choose the most appropriate derivative to hedge the exposure, and execute derivatives transactions. To understand this book, prior knowledge of derivatives is not necessary—only familiarity with finance.

People holding supervisory positions in banks and companies will benefit from reading this book. They do not need to know the details of how to execute transactions but do need to know if the transactions are appropriate to the type of exposure and if the proper controls are in place. Readers will learn why derivatives are a useful and necessary financial tool, and why people who use them inappropriately get their institutions into difficulty. Supervisors will certainly want to read the first five chapters and the chapters about derivative credit risk and interest rate exposure in banks. Although the other chapters are not more difficult, they are somewhat more detailed.

Mathematical formulas are used for illustration. If you are not comfortable with formulas, however, you can read around them; you will not miss the sense of what is being said.

Derivatives are tools. Before picking up a tool, you must take time to understand what you are building. Therefore Chapter 1 begins with a discussion of hedging interest rate exposure within the context of a bank's or company's overall objectives. Chapters 2 and 3 focus on how interest rate exposure occurs in companies and how to estimate its impact. Only then do we look at derivatives. With this foundation we look at ways to compare various hedging alternatives. Chapters 5 through 11 discuss different derivative products. All are considered in an exposure setting, and though most of the examples are from a company viewpoint, they apply equally to banks. This perspective enables bankers to see situations the way their customers do and thus provide better support. The focus is on derivatives that reduce risk without introducing additional risk.

Chapter 12, about the credit risk of derivatives, covers estimating it, reducing it, managing credit problems, and documenting transactions. The next two chapters are largely for bankers managing interest rate exposure in their own institutions. Banks have special exposure situations and use a number of specialized derivatives to address them. In Chapter 15 we walk through two transactions—from the exposure to booking the entries. The book ends with Descriptions of Derivative Products which cover a long list of products, many not mentioned in the text. It is explicit about those that hedge exposure and those that are used for taking a view on the direction of interest rates. Words italicized in the text are also found in the Descriptions of Derivative Products.

Throughout the book are a number of examples that compare one derivative solution to another and conclude which is the appropriate one to use. The conclusion is based on my assumptions about current and future rates and company circumstances. Examples are not intended to recommend a particular strategy. The method of analysis is the important lesson; different circumstances can lead to different conclusions.

Much of what I know about derivatives I learned from others. Bill Huth and Dick Turney, my colleagues at Bank of America, were particularly important in my education. They willingly shared with me their extensive experience and knowledge of the derivatives market. I also want to acknowledge the role of Galen Burghardt's instruction and writings. And thanks to Mike Joseph and Chris Karow for sharing their knowledge of accounting.

Special thanks go to Tim Bottoms for suggesting I write this book and Dave Coulter for giving me the opportunity to become involved in the derivatives market.

I am very grateful for the comments and suggestions of the reviewers: John Logan, Executive Vice President, First American National Bank; Dick Turney, Vice President, Financial Engineering and Risk Management, Bank of America; and John Wheatley, Managing Director, Capital Markets Group, First Union Corporation. They have been generous in their time and commitment to this book. I trust they will find their efforts have been worthwhile. They are not responsible for any errors or omissions; only I am.

My partner in this book has been Beverly Mills. Her special contributions have been to the clarity of the prose, continuity of thought, and practicality of application. What you will read is a product of our joint efforts.

San Francisco
January 1996

CHAPTER 1

HEDGING WITH DERIVATIVES

This book is a valuable tool for people in corporate treasury departments and their bankers who are interested in learning how to hedge interest rate exposure with derivatives. Before going further, we'll provide a definition for the two key terms. A *hedge* is an arrangement that offsets interest rate exposure or changes its character. *Derivatives* are financial instruments whose value or payout is tied to the price or rate on a more basic instrument, like a security or deposit.

The book also is addressed to bankers who are concerned with asset/liability management. The focus is on those derivatives that reduce interest rate exposure without introducing additional risk. When derivatives are used appropriately, companies and banks gain enormous additional flexibility in investing and funding. When derivatives are not used correctly, they can lead to large losses, like those at Proctor and Gamble and Gibson Greetings. The key to appropriate use of derivatives is understanding what they do and how they hedge interest rate exposure.

The information discussed here will enable treasurers and their bankers to better identify a company's interest rate exposures and to formulate and execute appropriate solutions involving derivatives. Bankers will be able to better identify interest rate exposure within their own institutions and be able to formulate and execute appropriate solutions involving derivatives. Readers also will gain an understanding of the credit implications of derivative products and interest rate exposure.

You hedge interest rate exposure because it helps you promote and achieve your core corporate objectives: increasing value and competitiveness. In addition, it gives you greater flexibility in choosing how to fund companies, how to fund banks, and how to invest.

Hedging increases the value of your company by making its income pattern more predictable. Investors place a higher value on a company whose income grows at a steady pace of 14 percent to 16 percent a year than one that is up 25 percent one year and up only 10 percent the next year. The higher valuation of companies with steady earnings can be seen in the stock market's price/earnings ratios. Income patterns become more predictable when interest expense and earnings are bounded by hedges. Clearly, this does not remove volatility due to changes in the buying patterns of customers or changes in production costs. But it pulls one important element, interest rate exposure, out of the company's cost structure and stabilizes it.

Hedging and derivatives increase competitiveness in two ways: (1) reducing interest rate exposure allows your company to focus its attention on its market; and (2) derivatives give your company another tool to use in pricing its product. Derivatives are especially powerful if your company finances the customers that buy your products or the distributors that store them. In developing hedging policies, many companies research what others in the same industry are doing. This useful exercise helps you develop ideas; however, unless the cost and revenue structures are the same, mimicking the industry is not necessarily the best thing to do.

HEDGING POLICY

The Comptroller of the Currency, the Group of Thirty, and other public spirited bodies have published guidance on hedging with derivatives. For management, they can be summarized in four steps:

- Understand what the exposures are and what derivatives do to them.
- Hire or train knowledgeable people to transact and track the hedges.
- Develop clear objectives and policies to guide those people.
- Establish an independent system that tells you how your risk profile is affected by what people are doing.

Chapters 2, 3 and 13 discuss interest rate exposure in companies and banks and how to measure it. Developing clear objectives and policies is critical since objectives measure the success of the hedging activity and guide the people executing the hedges. In developing hedging policies, management and the board of directors need to think about the following issues:

- context in which the policy is being developed
- specific objective to be achieved
- criteria for measuring achievement of the objective
- amount of discretion delegated to the treasury department
- types of exposures to be hedged
- derivatives they are comfortable with

CONTEXT OF A HEDGING POLICY

A hedging policy should be different for every bank and company because each differs in terms of

- management experience
- amount of risk in other parts of the business
- industry
- competitive position
- financial health
- global position
- ability to invest in systems and control procedures

A company with a financially sophisticated and experienced management generally will tolerate larger interest rate exposures and use sophisticated derivatives. These companies feature an infrastructure that administers and monitors derivatives activity. Community banks will generally have less interest rate risk than regional banks, so their hedging policies will be simpler and they will use basic derivative products. Companies carrying considerable business risk in their day-to-day operations—film companies, high technology firms, new businesses—tolerate little interest rate exposure. Firms that are not financially healthy generally tolerate less interest rate risk and tend to use standard derivatives structures to accomplish their objectives. The discussion of these few factors points up the need to review hedging policies often. Companies change as people move out and new people move in to senior management And the risk profile changes as the company enters new markets, produces new products, or buys other businesses.

The amount of interest rate risk and the sophistication of the derivatives a company uses should mirror the sophistication of the systems and procedures used to measure exposure and track the effectiveness of the hedges. If it is the policy of a company or bank to use derivatives to reduce interest rate risk, the systems should be capable of determining that the derivatives transactions reduce risk. System and control procedure sophistication should lead, not follow, the sophistication of the derivatives being used and the size of the exposure being managed, so you should be prepared to invest the time and money to get the systems and control side *right*.

OBJECTIVES OF A HEDGE POLICY

The objectives of a hedge policy must be clear and unambiguous. Some objectives used by companies are to

- minimize financial expense
- minimize the economic value of debt
- reduce the risk of large increases in interest expense
- minimize accounting gains or losses
- maintain the net interest margin

The pursuit of each of these objectives leads to distinctly different actions. A company wanting to minimize financial expense may enter into transactions with the objective of generating earnings to offset interest expense. A company wanting to minimize the variation in interest expense would follow a more conservative approach, but this could easily lead to a higher expense level.

DISCRETION

A company's or bank's board of directors decides how much flexibility to allow management in hedging and derivative activities. Two aspects of the policy are (1) the extent that treasury people can decide the mix of floating and fixed rate debt and (2) the extent that the interest rate exposures of the investment portfolio are considered to offset exposures on the liability side. Company policy also should spell out whether treasury people have total discretion to be all fixed or all floating, or if the tolerance limits are 50 percent to 100 percent or 80 percent to 100 percent fixed rate.

TYPES OF EXPOSURES

The consequences of interest rate exposure can be immediate or far ranging. We look at three approaches to it: cash, value, and strategic.

The cash view is an immediate, today-oriented approach. It asks: What is the company earning on its assets? What is it paying on its liabilities? The difference in the two rates is reflected in the company's income statement.

The value view is future oriented. It is concerned with the effects of rate changes on the value of all future interest and principal flows. This approach takes current market rates and asks what someone would pay today for the cash flows from the short term investments, and what would the company have to pay someone to buy the cash flows on the bond. Today's answer to this question is compared to yesterday's answer. The difference is accounted for in the income statement today.

The economic view, a more strategic approach, looks at what competitors are paying for money. It asks: How does this affect your competitive position? What is the effect of interest rates on sales and production costs? What is the effect of a rise in interest rates on the company you buy raw materials from? What happens to your customers' ability to buy from you when rates rise? And if you are a bank, what happens to your consumer deposits when rates fall?

To develop a complete picture of its exposure, a company

needs to take all three views into account. In the short run, if cash flow is not positive, the company becomes insolvent. In the long run, if competitive, production, and sales effects are not considered, the company may go out of business. At the same time, a board of directors will probably decide to allocate management responsibility for each of the three viewpoints separately, perhaps reserving decisions on hedging economic exposure for itself.

DERIVATIVE INSTRUMENTS

A hedging policy should specify the derivatives to be used. They should be derivatives that management and the board understand. Possible variations are to

- transact derivatives on an exchange, for example, futures, or with a bank, for example, swaps
- use standard derivative structures, for example, swaps, caps, floors, futures contracts
- buy and sell options, for example, collars, corridors, or buy only
- enter into derivatives that involve leverage, for example, inverse floating rate notes

CONTROLS AND REPORTING

The most important part of the hedging policy is the control and reporting structure that accompanies it. Most of the 1994 and 1995 news stories about the problems with derivatives might have been more appropriately titled: "the problems with internal control." This clearly applies to Barings in Singapore and to Orange County, California. Many companies and banks engaged in derivatives before they had basic controls in place. The willingness to use derivatives to hedge interest rate exposure must be accompanied by the willingness to invest the time and money to set up a professional internal control infrastructure.

Segregation of duties is the most basic tenet of control. For the following functions, people and reporting lines should be separated:

- execution of transactions
- analysis and monitoring of hedging results
- confirmation and settlement of transactions
- accounting

For each discretionary element, levels of authority need to be established for:

- maturity of derivatives transactions
- derivatives used (including what constitutes a new derivative)
- counterparty exposure limits
- types of exposure hedged
- amounts of individual transactions (including total amount)

After establishing the authorities, communicate them to your regular counterparties. A letter on trading terms and conditions would identify those authorized to enter into transactions for the company, the types of derivatives they can transact, and their trading limits, amounts, and tenors. The letter also would be explicit about the derivatives the company will not enter into. Additionally, include a section on procedures for settling differences that may arise on the terms of a transaction done over the phone.

The frequency of reporting depends on the consequences of interest rate exposure to the firm. In no event should reporting be less frequent than once a month. Items that need to be reported to senior management and the board of directors are:

- previously identified exposures
- hedges against those exposures
- performance of the hedges, on a stand-alone basis, on an accounting basis and on a mark to market basis. (It is vital that the rates and prices used in valuing the hedges be sourced from outside the company.)
- performance of the hedges, together with the exposures, on accounting and mark to market bases and on a tax-effective basis
- new exposures
- effect on the firm of changes in interest rates
- counterparty exposure, actual and potential
- new regulatory, legal, tax, and on accounting issues

SOURCES

Controller of the Currency, "Risk Management of Financial Derivatives," *Banking Issuance*, BC-277, October 27, 1993 and "Questions and Answers—Re: BC-277," *OCC Bulletin*, May 10, 1994.

Global Derivatives Study Group, *Derivatives: Practices and Principles*, Washington, DC, Group of Thirty, July 1993.

Tanya Styblo Beder, "Updating Risk Management to Control Losses," in Jess Lederman and Robert A. Klein, ed., *Financial Engineering with Derivatives*, New York, Irwin Professional Publishing, 1995, pp. 167- 182.

Robert Mark, "Beyond Value at Risk," *Derivatives Strategy,* Vol. 4, No. 14, October 2, 1995, pp. 3-5.

J. Chris Karow, *Treasury and Risk Management Services,* Ernst & Young LLP, 1995.

Treasury Management Association, *Voluntary Principles and Practices Guidelines for End-Users of Derivatives*, Bethesda, MD, Treasury Management Association, 1995.

CHAPTER 2

How Interest Rate Exposure Occurs in Companies

When you borrow or invest money, cash flows result from interest and principal payments or interest and principal receipts. Because rates are volatile, cash flows can vary. As you know, interest rate risk can have favorable consequences, since investment returns rise as interest rates rise. And it can have unfavorable consequences, because interest payments rise as rates rise.

We'll begin our look at derivatives by showing how interest rate exposure is a natural result of your financial decisions. In this chapter, we'll examine the effect of interest rate exposure on your cash flow and on the value of your assets and liabilities. We present a wide range of exposures, gathered from many different types of companies, to give you a wide perspective on the issues. Understanding exposure is the foundation for knowing how to select the appropriate derivative.

THE EFFECT ON CASH FLOW

Your cash flows are affected by the amount of financial liabilities and assets you have, the movement of interest rates, and how long a given rate is in effect. Let's look at several transactions and see how they create different types of exposure—floating rate, fixed rate, and a combination of fixed and floating rate.

FLOATING RATE EXPOSURE

Let's say you take out a one-year loan. You agree to pay interest every three months and repay the principal at the end of the year. If interest rates rise over the course of the year, your interest expense rises. If rates fall over the course of the year, you benefit from lower interest expense.

In another transaction, you borrow from your bank at the prime rate to finance inventory. Interest is paid every 90 days. The prime rate, however, changes about once every 143 days (the average for the period January 1990 and July 1995). In thinking about interest rate risk, the most relevant point in time is when you become subject to a rate change, not when the interest bill is paid.

FIXED RATE EXPOSURE

To construct an addition to your plant, you borrow from an insurance company at a fixed rate for 10 years. Every six months you will pay out a fixed amount of interest to the lender; therefore, you do not have any risk that your interest bill will rise over the period of the loan. Regardless of rate movements, you will not pay less. And if you attempted to prepay the fixed rate loan when interest rates fell, you would probably have a prepayment penalty.

FIXED AND FLOATING RATE EXPOSURE

Your company recently floated a long term,fixed rate bond in the European market to finance an acquisition. Pending the acquisition, you invest the money in 30-day commercial paper. In the short run, a rise in rates will help your company; a fall will result in less income.

In another example, as part of your company's marketing program, customers' purchases are financed at a fixed rate for up to five years. You finance the loan program by issuing commercial paper. You, therefore, are exposed to a movement of short term interest rates, while the rate on the customer loans is fixed. If commercial paper rates rise, the financing margin will be squeezed. If rates fall, company income will rise.

THE EFFECT ON VALUE

We've seen how a change in rates affects cash flows and consequently has an immediate effect on the bottom line. In addition, these rate changes affect the value of your company. Let's look at some examples of how rates affect the value of your financial assets and your competitive position. When you borrowed at a fixed rate of 9 percent for 10 years, the movement of interest rates for the next 10 years has no affect on cash flows. The movement of rates does, however, affect the value of the bond you issued. If long term interest rates rise, your 9 percent bond becomes more valuable to your company. It would have to pay a higher rate today to borrow on the same terms. The lower rate bond, therefore, becomes more valuable in the higher interest rate environment. Also your company is in a potentially better position regarding competitors, who may have borrowed at floating rates, or who waited to issue long term debt.

On the other hand, if your portfolio contains fixed rate customer loans, they become less valuable as long term interest rates rise. In the new interest rate environment, you would be able to charge a higher rate on these loans. The portfolio's decline in value also affects your firm's value as a whole. In addition, your company has less financial flexibility than competitors who financed equipment sales on a floating rate basis.

The value of your bond and customer loan portfolio, in a new interest rate environment, depends on the amount of the rate change, the maturity of the financial instruments, and the pattern of the cash flows. The effect on value is greater the more rates change, the longer the time to maturity, and when the interest cash flows occur toward the end of the instrument's life. Clearly the size of a rate change directly affects the size of the value change. Longer maturity has a direct effect, because any change in rates affects a greater number of cash flows. The pattern of the interest flows affects value, because the effect of any rate change increases more than proportionately over time. In Illustration 2.1, which shows these effects, the lines would be steeper if the interest flows were weighted towards the end of the life of the instrument.

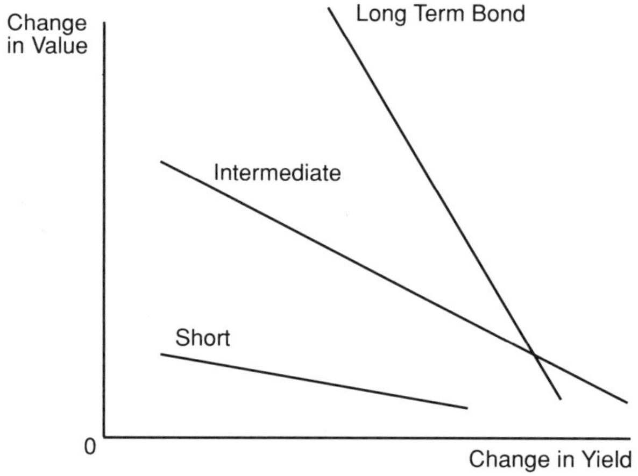

Illustration 2.1 Effect on Value

Source: Adapted from illustrations by Kenneth R. Kapner and John F. Marshall, *The Swaps Handbook,* New York, New York Institute of Finance, 1990, p. 141.

DURATION

How do you measure the sensitivity of financial instruments to changes in interest rates? What are the capabilities or limitations of these measures? The most useful ways to measure a change in value are duration and dollar value of a basis point. Although duration is a measure of the average life of a bond (or any fixed rate financial instrument), you can use it to deduce the effect of a change in rate.

The measure was first developed by Frederick Macaulay in 1938. Macaulay's contribution was to take the weighted average maturity measure of a bond's life and put all of the cash flows in today's terms before weighting them by the year they occurred. To illustrate the concept, let's assume your company invests $100,000,000 in a bond that carries an interest rate of 10 percent, payable annually, principal payable at maturity, with a term of five years.

The yearly cash flow stream (in dollars) is:

Year 1	Year 2	Year 3	Year 4	Year 5
10,000,000	10,000,000	10,000,000	10,000,000	110,000,000

Weighted average maturity weights each cash flow by the number of the year it occurs and divides by the sum of all the cash flows. (For the examples we will drop 000,000.)

Year 1	Year 2	Year 3	Year 4	Year 5
$\frac{10 \times 1}{150}$	$\frac{10 \times 2}{150}$	$\frac{10 \times 3}{150}$	$\frac{10 \times 4}{150}$	$\frac{110 \times 5}{150}$

The weighted average maturity is 4.33 years.

The duration measure puts the cash flows in today's terms before weighting them by the years. To do that, it is necessary to adjust the cash flows by a discount factor. The appropriate discount factor for each year is different, reflecting differences in rates in each year. In this example, the rates start at 6 percent in Year 1 and go to 10 percent in Year 5, in 1 percent steps.

Year 1	Year 2	Year 3	Year 4	Year 5
$\frac{10}{1.06}$	$\frac{10}{1.07\text{^}2}$	$\frac{10}{1.08\text{^}3}$	$\frac{10}{1.09\text{^}4}$	$\frac{110}{1.10\text{^}5}$
9.4348	8.734	7.938	7.084	68.301

The sum of these cash flows is 101.49

Duration weights today's value of the cash flows by the year they occur and divides by their sum, just as the weighted average maturity does with the unadjusted flows.

Year 1	Year 2	Year 3	Year 4	Year 5
$\frac{9.434 \times 1}{101.49}$	$\frac{8.734 \times 2}{101.49}$	$\frac{7.938 \times 3}{101.49}$	$\frac{7.084 \times 4}{101.49}$	$\frac{68.301 \times 5}{101.49}$

The duration of the company's five-year finance paper is 4.14 years.

The duration number makes it possible to calculate the impact of small changes in rates on the value of the financial instrument. Formula:

[Value of the bond × change in rate × duration] / (1 + rate/2)

As applied to the company
[100,000,000 × 1% × 4.14] / (1 + .10/2)
A 1 percent rise in rates across the board would decrease the value of the bond by $3,942,857.

The general formula for duration is:

The sum of the present value of future cash flows weighted by the time they occur divided by the sum of the present value of all the flows (unweighted).

The general formula for duration in symbols is:

$$D = \frac{\sum_{t=1}^{N} t \times \frac{F(t)}{(1 + R(t))^{\wedge}t}}{\sum_{t=1}^{N} \frac{F(t)}{(1 + R(t))^{\wedge}t}}$$

where	t	=	year or period
	F(t)	=	cash flow in year t
	R(t)	=	discount rate applied to year t
	N	=	maturity of the instrument
	D	=	duration, in years

DOLLAR VALUE OF A BASIS POINT

The dollar value of a basis point is the second method for easily assessing change in the value of a financial instrument. A basis point is 1/100 of 1 percent or 0.0001. The measure derives from the relation between price and yield of a fixed rate instrument. A basis point change in yield affects a bond with a low yield much more than it affects a bond with a high yield. In Illustration

2.2, the bond represented by point **a'** has a lower yield than the bond represented by **c'**. The distance between **a** and **b** represents one basis point. The associated difference in price, or value, is represented by the distance between **a'** and **b'**. The distance between **c** and **d** also represents one basis point. The associated difference in price is represented by the distance between **c'** and **d'**. Clearly the distance between **a'** and **b'** is greater than the distance between **c'** and **d'**.

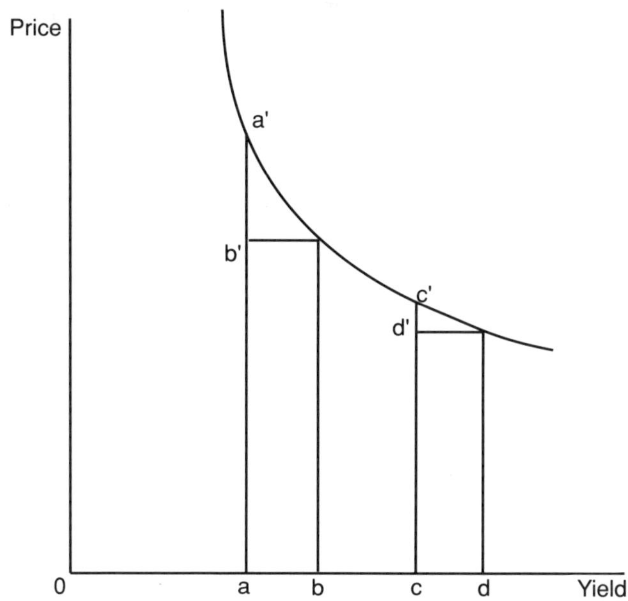

Illustration 2.2 Low Yield versus High Yield

Source: Adapted from illustrations by Frank J. Fabozzi, *Fixed Income Mathematics,* Chicago, Probus Publishing Company, 1993, pp. 142-143.

A basis point change in yield also affects a bond with a long maturity more than it affects a bond with a short maturity. The price/yield curve, noted as F in Illustration 2.3, has a longer maturity than the one noted as E. The change from **a** to **b** represents a one basis point change in yield. The change in price, or value, is greater for bond F than it is for bond E; the change from **a'** to **b'** is greater than the change from **a"** to **b"**.

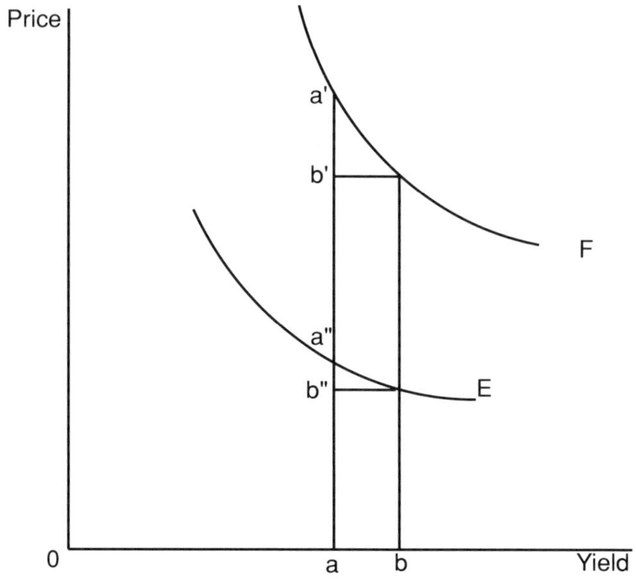

Illustration 2.3 Long Maturity versus Short Maturity

The change is usually expressed in terms of a million dollars. For example, for a five-year bond yielding 10 percent, the dollar value of a basis point is $379. If a bond with the same yield has a 15-year maturity, the value of a basis point is $760. (This assumes the bonds have a coupon of 10 percent and current market rate levels are 10 percent.)

You calculate the dollar value of a basis point by calculating the price of a bond twice: first, assuming one rate level; second, assuming a rate level that differs by one basis point. Whether or not the change is up or down makes only a small difference for long maturities and high yields.

Formula:

$$P = \sum_{t=1}^{N} \frac{C}{(1+R)^{\wedge}t} + \frac{M}{(1+R)^{\wedge}N}$$

$$P = \sum_{t=1}^{N} \frac{C}{(1+R+.0001)^{\wedge}t} + \frac{M}{(1=R+.0001)^{\wedge}N}$$

Dollar value of a basis point = P − P'

where P = price in dollars

t = year

C = coupon on the bond

R = current market interest rate for the maturity

N = number of periods

M = maturity value

SUMMARY OF THE EFFECTS ON CASH FLOW AND VALUE

Table 2.1 summarizes the effects of rates on borrowers and investors. Note that any change in interest rates has the same effect on the investor in fixed rate assets as it has on the company that borrows at a floating rate. Similarly, the investor in floating rate assets will be affected the same as the company that borrows at a fixed rate.

Table 2.1 Effects of Rates

Effect	**Investors**		**Borrowers**	
	Fixed Rate	**Floating Rate**	**Fixed Rate**	**Floating Rate**
Cash Flow				
Rates up	none	positive	none	negative
Rates down	none	negative	none	positive
Value				
Rates up	negative	none	positive	none
Rates down	positive	none	negative	none

CHAPTER 3

How to Quantify the Impact of Exposure

So far we have identified the circumstances in which exposure occurs in companies. We now look at ways to quantify the impacts of interest rate change and volatility on the income and value of a company. If you have a good grasp of your company's interest rate sensitivity, you can design and choose appropriate hedges. We'll first look at a static analysis of a company's exposure, look at an analysis that incorporates future plans, look at the effects of interest changes on a company's sales and pricing, and finally, look at a number of ways to model interest rate movements.

STATIC GAP

Banks have used gap analysis to measure interest rate sensitivity for many years. This analysis is equally applicable to nonfinancial companies. Basically the process is to review the assets, liabilities, and equity account, and identify items with interest rates. These items are put in a "maturity bucket" according to when the rate on the item will change. A note that will mature in two years is placed in the two-year bucket, because it is assumed that it will be replaced by another note at a different rate. Assets that re-price in a given bucket are compared to liabilities that re-price in the same bucket. They are termed rate sensitive assets (RSA) and rate sensitive liabilities (RSL). The net of the two is the rate sensitivity in that maturity bucket.

Let's look at a sample gap statement. Say your company has interests in household durable goods, patent drugs, and consumer finance. You have cash and short term investments of $850 million in bank deposits, commercial paper, government agencies notes, and preferred stock. You finance the sales of household durable goods with installment loans at a fixed rate for up to five years and the sales of patent drugs on the company credit card. Notes receivable were generated recently from the sale of a subsidiary. The liability and equity side of the balance sheet are fairly straight forward. Table 3.1 shows the static gap report. Most of it is generated from the company's published financial reports: balance sheet, income statement, statement of changes in financial position, and notes to the financial statement.

Minus signs in the gap row mean that you have more liabilities than assets re-pricing in a maturity bucket. Thus you are exposed to a rise in interest rates. A positive number means that you have more assets than liabilities re-pricing in a maturity bucket. Therefore you are exposed to a fall in interest rates. The gap report shows that your company is exposed to a rise in short rates over the next year. But for the following three years, you are exposed to a fall in interest rates. You *now* know that you need to design different hedge programs for different periods.

This report does not reveal two important pieces of information: what happens if the future is not a replica of the past (discussed below in Dynamic Gap), and what rates the company is exposed to. When we talk about what rates the company is exposed to, the reference is to the part of the yield curve that affects your company. It makes a difference whether a company is affected by an increase in three-month rates or five-year rates. Later in this chapter we will address this issue.

Table 3.1 Static Gap

Period	**0-30 days**	**31-90 days**	**91-180 days**	**181-365 days**	**1 to 2 years**	**2 to 3 years**	**3 to 5 years**	**5+ years**
Assets								
Deposits	100							
CP		200						
Agencies					250			
Preferred stock			300					
Credit card receivables					400			
Customer loans		40	90	200	450	500	800	25
Notes receivable					75	75	150	
Total RSA	**100**	**240**	**390**	**200**	**1175**	**575**	**950**	**25**
Liabilities & Equity								
CP	650	300						
Bank loans			400					
Medium term			100	200	100	100	200	
Long term notes				50				600
Preferred stock		300						
Total RSL	**650**	**600**	**500**	**250**	**100**	**100**	**200**	**600**
Gap	**–550**	**–360**	**–110**	**–50**	**1075**	**475**	**750**	**–575**
Cumulative	**–550**	**–910**	**–1020**	**–1070**	**5**	**480**	**1230**	**675**

DYNAMIC GAP

A dynamic gap report takes into account your company's plans and capital structure objectives still on the drawing board. Among the plans might be to decrease the debt/equity ratio by retiring debt or issuing equity (common, preferred, or convertible debt), increase asset liquidity, alter the mix of fixed and floating liabilities, increase term debt, and change the mix of senior to subordinated debt.

The company's plans include plant expansions, major projects, acquisitions, and divestitures. The impact on your company's interest rate risk profile depends on how expansions, projects, and acquisitions are financed, or how the proceeds from the sale of a subsidiary are used. Financing possibilities and their potential effect on interest rate exposure are:

Stock: If preferred stock, it can carry a fixed or floating rate.

Cash: Bank loans are usually floating rate. Bonds may be fixed or floating. Leases are usually fixed rate.

War Chest: If taken from cash and investments on hand, it will reduce short term, rate sensitive assets.

Notes to the Seller: May be fixed or floating.

A company may buy the assets or the assets and liabilities of another company. Whichever the company purchases, the interest rate exposure of the combined entity will be different after the combination.

Selling a subsidiary or a line of business has different effects, depending on what is sold (assets or assets and liabilities) as well as what is received for the sale: stock, cash, or notes. If cash, it can be used to pay off fixed or floating rate debt or be invested in fixed or floating rate paper. Notes can be fixed or floating rate.

To generate a dynamic gap report, you need to look forward not only to these major future events but also to the evolution of the businesses your company is in. The process entails generating gap reports at various points in the future, then linking them to observe the exposure pattern. Illustration 3.1 shows how this might look for your company for the next two years. Included are the major plant and marketing expansion plans that you intend to finance, initially, by increasing the commercial paper program and bank borrowing.

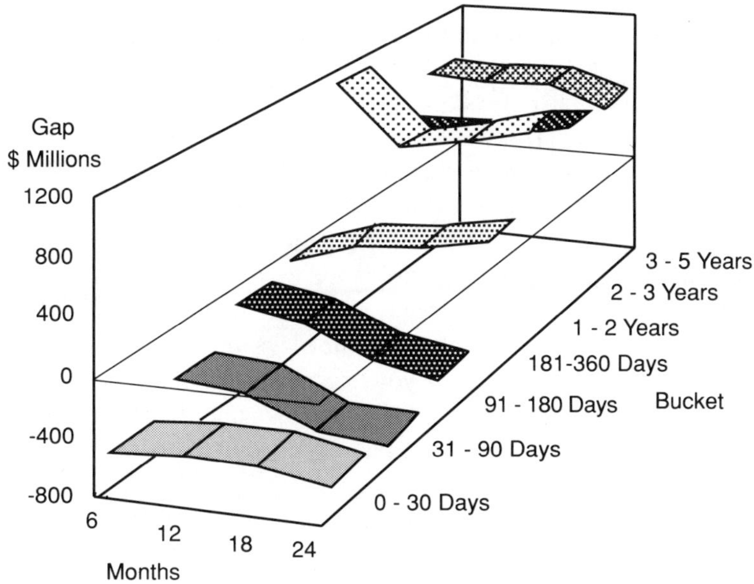

Illustration 3.1 Dynamic Gap

Illustration 3.1 shows that, for the forecast period, the company will remain exposed to increases in short term interest rates, and become increasingly so. The lines for the first three buckets are negative for the entire period.

MEASUREMENT OF ECONOMIC EXPOSURE

Interest rate movement does more to a company than affect the cash flows and values of financial instruments. It affects all aspects of the business. Let's say your company finances the purchase of the household durable goods it manufactures. If interest rates rise, your customers will pay more in finance charges and, as a result, will probably buy fewer refrigerators and stoves. In addition, when interest rates rise, fewer new homes are purchased or built, thereby reducing the demand for these items. Another effect comes through your company's suppliers. If companies that provide sheet aluminum, plastic, and electrical equipment are leveraged, there will be pressure to increase prices. Even though the accounting values of your company's nonfinancial assets are not affected, their economic values will be. The bottom line is that you need to assess the effect of rates on the entire firm and not only on the financial assets and liabilities.

Multivariate regression analysis is one way of assessing the effect of the influence of interest rates. This statistical analysis enables a company to separate the influence of different variables that affect income, such as interest rates, commodity prices, foreign exchange rates, or consumer confidence, and assign a level of importance to each. Data are collected on all of the relevant variables, at least quarterly, through a number of business cycles. If you find that the level of interest rates plays an overwhelming role in explaining the changes in your company's income, you might want to fix all borrowing costs. By doing so, the company does not suffer from both increased interest expense and slow sales when interest rates rise.

In some industries, higher interest rates lead to higher net income. Union Carbide, one of the pioneers in the use of multivariate regression analysis, found that to be the case.[1] Few generalities, however, apply to industries or companies. Each company must do its own analysis. Depending on the complexity of the company and the number of markets it serves, it may be desirable to break the analysis out by revenues and expenses, or by business segment. A company's patent drug business is certainly affected by different variables than its household durable goods business.

MODELING INTEREST RATE MOVEMENTS

Short, medium, and long term interest rates tend to move up and down together, but rarely by the same amount. Illustration 3.2 shows the changes in the relationships between three-month, five-year, and 30-year rates over the last 16 years, as they have moved up and down. When interest rates are at their cyclical highs, the spreads between different maturities are most compressed. As rates bottom out, spreads are widest. Most ways of modeling interest rate movement focus on one specific rate—three-month, six-month, or five-year. It is useful to look at models that show a family of rates and shifts in the relationships between them.

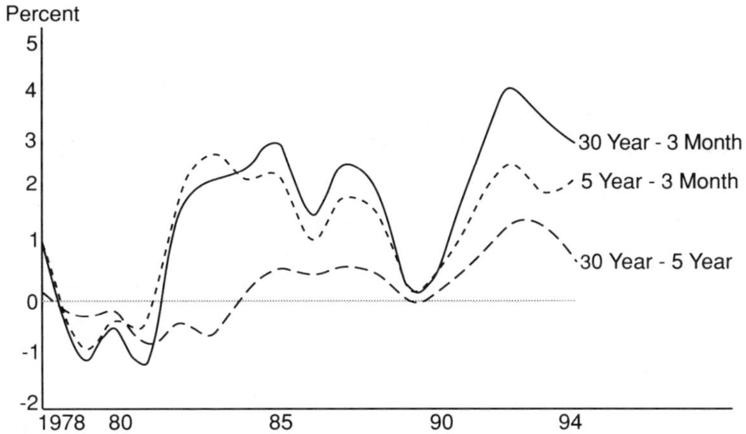

Illustration 3.2 Movement of Interest Rates and Rate Differentials

Sources: The rates used in the graphs are U.S. Treasury yields. Data are from V.K. Ranganathan, *Interest Rate Trends & Comparisons,* New York, Bank of America, 1995, pp. 101, 172, 175.

RATE FORECASTS

In addition to its internal forecasts, there are a number of places a company can obtain interest rate forecasts. The economics departments of commercial and investment banks forecast interest rates. Many people use the market itself as a forecaster of interest rates. Those that subscribe to the expectations theory of the yield curve suggest that forward rates are the collective judgment of market participants on where rates will be in the future. As we will see in Chapter 6, a series of forward rates can be constructed for any maturity, for example, from three months to 10 years. And conveniently, Eurodollar futures contracts provide the forward rates for three-month money. Futures contracts are covered more fully in Chapter 7.

BINOMIAL RATE MODEL

When a single rate forecast is used, it is relatively easy to look at the assumptions being made. The binomial rate model and the Monte Carlo simulation make a few crucial assumptions and generate a lot of numbers and statistics. It pays to fully understand the assumptions being made with these models before being guided by them.

The binomial model starts with today's rate, say 7.50 percent. Three months from now, the rate will have gone up or gone down, and though we are not sure which way it will have gone, we're willing to assign some probabilities to each event. Also we estimate how much the rate will go up or down by looking at the historical volatility of the rate. We do this for subsequent periods. At the end of the process, we have a lattice of interest rates, each with a probability attached to it. It is possible to choose any time interval desired—a week, a month, three months. The probabilities of the rate going up or going down can be set at the beginning or altered at each stage. The rate of increase and decrease can be estimated separately.

The critical inputs for the binomial model are: (1) the probability of a rate going up from where it is, and conversely, the probability of the rate going down and (2) the amount by which the rate goes up and goes down in the specified time period. In Illustration 3.3, the first lattice shows interest rates, the one below shows probabilities of the rate being attained in that period. The top right node of the first lattice has 10.20 percent as one of the possible interest rates in that period. The lattice below ascribes an 83 percent probability of that rate occurring. In the top lattice, the interest rate 9.19 percent is estimated to have a 16 percent probability of occurring.

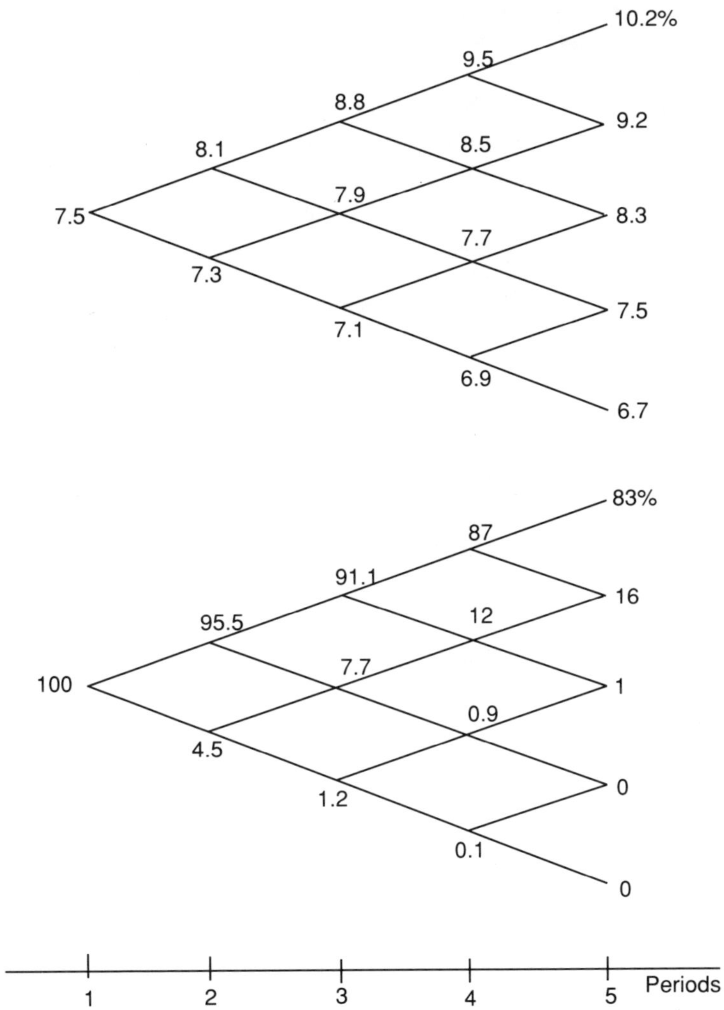

Illustration 3.3 Binomial Rate Model

Increasingly, variations of the binomial rate model are being used to estimate the path of future interest rates and to price derivatives. These variations show more than two ways a rate can move from a given starting point. A trinomial model has three possibilities; a rate could go up, down, or stay the same. It has been further extended to five possibilities for a rate. The reason for the extensions is to examine more possibilities by producing a denser lattice. The principles behind the extensions and the assumptions of these multinomial models are the same as the binomial model.

MONTE CARLO SIMULATION

The Monte Carlo simulation is based on the premise that the path of future interest rates is unknown. But we can count on certain properties about interest rates:

- The further in the future we forecast, the less accurate we are.
- Nominal interest rates do not go lower than zero.
- Interest rates are positively correlated.

Given these properties, the Monte Carlo technique requires that (1) a trend be specified, (2) upper and lower bounds for rates be established, and (3) the volatility of rates, based either on their historical movement or implied in current option prices, be set. The simulation then generates thousands of interest rate paths. These paths are then used to value an exposure or a derivative transaction. Individual values are not of particular interest, but their distribution is.

Illustration 3.4 shows the distribution of predicted rates around the current futures curve for the next five years. The band describes where 68 percent, or one standard deviation, of the simulated curves falls. It widens as time goes on, and has an upward drift because the Eurodollar futures curve is upward sloping.

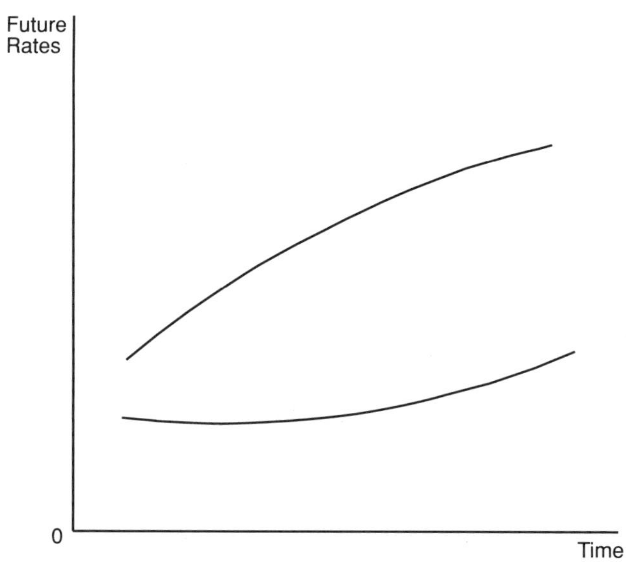

Illustration 3.4 Monte Carlo Simulation, Distribution of Results

Binomial and trinomial models are used more frequently than Monte Carlo simulation. One reason is time. A trinomial model produces results in minutes; a Monte Carlo simulation takes hours, although the technology is improving. Additionally the binomial and trinomial models produce equivalent results when examining the effects of rates on exposure and evaluating the value of most derivatives. Only derivatives whose value depends on what happened in a previous period need to be valued with a Monte Carlo simulation.

GAP AND RATE MODELS

In quantifying its exposure to interest rate risk, the level of detail a company will go to depends on the complexity of the company. A company with three separate business lines and $10 billion in sales makes fewer simplifying assumptions than a company with one line of business and $250 million in sales.

At the greatest level of detail, a company produces dynamic gap schedules classified according to the segment of the yield curve to which they were exposed. For example, one schedule for the five-year area encompasses the customer loan portfolio and medium term debt. A second schedule, in the 30- to 180-day area, includes most of the company's investments, its commercial paper program, and bank loans. Then, using one of the rate modeling methods, the company generates projections of future rates for each segment of the yield curve: three months, six months, five years. Putting together these schedules and rate projections will quantify the company's exposure to interest rates from its financial instruments.

On a broader scale, a company's economic exposure to interest rates also can be generated using the results of the regression analysis and rate projections. Kapner and Marshall show a convenient way to visualize the combination of a Monte Carlo simulation and regression analysis. In Illustration 3.5, the diagram on the left shows the relation between interest rates and the income of a company. Rising interest rates negatively impact income. The center diagram shows the distribution of rates that resulted from a Monte Carlo simulation. The diagram on the right combines the two and shows the effect on the company's income in a range that includes 95 percent of the simulated interest rate scenarios. If the company finds the income variation too large, its response will be to use derivatives and other alternatives to make the company less sensitive to rates. In terms of the Illustration, the company will attempt to flatten the line relating rates to income.

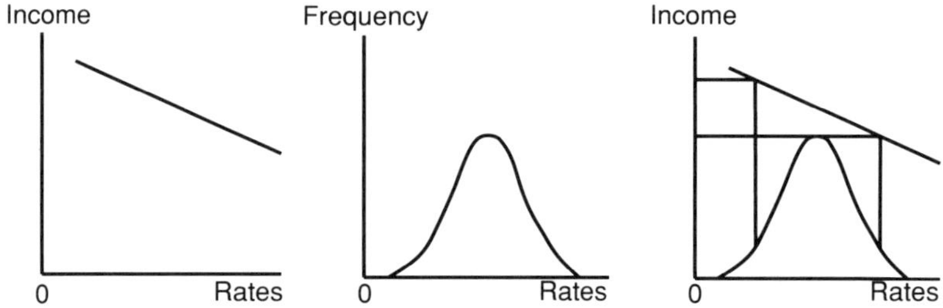

Illustration 3.5 Combination of Regression and Monte Carlo Simulation

Source: Adapted from Kenneth R. Kapner and John F. Marshall, *The Swaps Handbook,* New York, New York Institute of Finance, 1990, pp. 148-153 .

NOTE

1. Elayne Sheridan, "Smarter than the Average Payer," *RISK*, Vol. 5, No. 11, December 1992, pp. 76-78.

CHAPTER 4

Alternatives for Hedging Exposure

In Chapters 2 and 3, we looked at the interest rate exposure created by borrowing, investing, acquisition, and expansion plans. In this chapter, we'll take a broad look at the alternatives available to you for hedging the exposure. Subsequent chapters will go into greater detail.

A hedge is an arrangement to offset and change the character of interest rate exposure. The six alternatives discussed below produce the offset in different ways, but generally fall into two camps: symmetric, when the hedge locks the company into a specific rate regardless of what happens to market interest rates, and asymmetric, when the company is allowed to choose the contract rate or the market, rate, whichever is the most favorable.[1] Asymmetric hedges provide insurance: you are compensated if things go wrong; nothing happens if things go right. Although some of the six alternatives are not derivatives, they are included because they may be more appropriate for particular exposure situations. Derivatives are one way, but not always the only or best way, to hedge an exposure. Chapter 5 specifically addresses how to choose among alternatives by establishing criteria for a good hedge.

SELL/RETIRE

If a company is not comfortable with the exposure generated by a bond it holds, it can always sell the bond and use the proceeds to buy another investment that better fits its current interest rate risk appetite. Likewise with a loan, the company can repay a floating rate loan with the proceeds of a fixed rate bond issue. In these instances, the company extinguishes its exposure by selling or retiring the instrument that generated it. It then substitutes another instrument more to its liking. This is a symmetric hedge.

For example, if you fund consumer installment loans with commercial paper, you could retire the paper and issue medium term notes. The maturities of the medium term notes are a better offset for the interest rate exposure generated by the loans.

Retiring a loan and selling an asset usually cannot be done overnight. New borrowing arrangements need to be set up, and time is needed to arrange a medium term note program. If you had a loan from an insurance company, it would take time to negotiate the prepayment fee. On the asset side, although you may like the credit quality of your investment, you may not quickly find one of similar quality with the same return.

FORWARD RATE AGREEMENT

A *forward rate agreement* (FRA) is an interest rate contract that fixes a rate for a single period in the future on a given amount of money. In an earlier example, you took out a one-year loan where the interest rate reset every three months. Let's say you are now two months away from the next reset day. Fearing that the Federal Reserve is going to raise rates, you want to fix the rate for the coming three-month period today. This requires a transaction that has two legs. On the first leg, you agree to pay a bank (the lending bank or another) 6.25 percent for the three-month period. On the second leg, the bank agrees to pay you whatever the three-month rate is on the reset day. This agreement is shown in Illustration 4.1. The first line shows your floating rate exposure two months ahead (floating rates are denoted by white arrows, fixed rates are denoted by gray arrows). The second line shows the agreement with the bank. The two variable cash flows net one another, and you effectively pay the fixed rate.

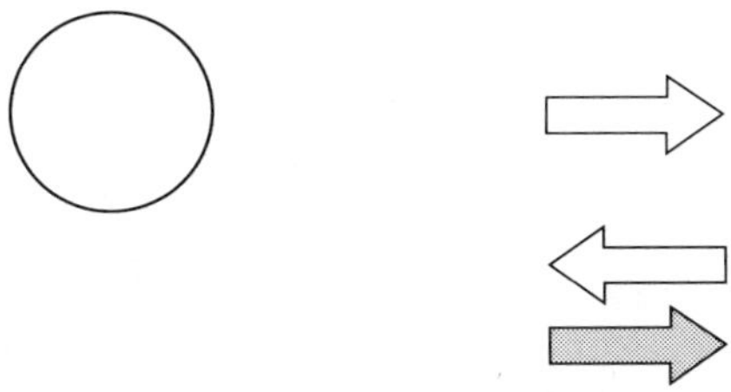

Illustration 4.1 Forward Rate Agreement

You were right about rates, they went up to seven percent. When it came time to settle:

You pay:	7%	on the loan
You pay:	6.25%	on first leg of the FRA
You receive:	7%	on second leg of the FRA
Your net rate:	**6.25%**	

As we said, an FRA is a contract that fixes a rate for a single period in the future on a given amount of money. It is a symmetric hedge, so with interest rates at 7 percent you paid 6.25 percent. If you were wrong about the direction of interest rates, and they had fallen to 5 percent, you would still pay 6.25 percent:

You pay:	5%	on the one year loan
You pay:	6.25%	on first leg of the FRA
You receive:	5%	on second leg of the FRA
Your net rate:	**6.25**%	

FUTURES

An interest rate futures contract fixes an interest rate in the future the same as an FRA, but with a significant difference: interest rate futures contracts have only four settlement days a year, whereas FRAs can be contracted for any business day. This introduces a timing risk for the company. As shown in Illustration 4.2, the futures contract may settle before (or after) the reset day of the loan. If rates move between the futures settlement day and the interest rate reset day, the offset will be less than perfect.

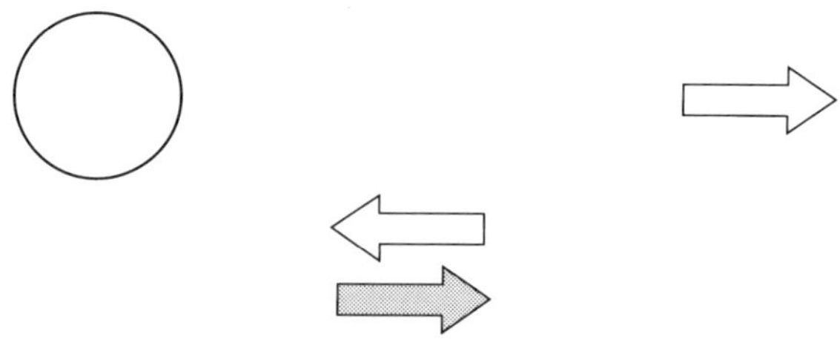

Illustration 4.2 Futures

SWAP

A *swap* is an arrangement that a company makes with a commercial or investment bank to exchange interest payments over a defined period of time. The payments are calculated on the basis of an agreed principal amount and interest rate indices. Let's consider a company borrowing at a floating rate. This is shown in the top line of Illustration 4.3. The second line shows the inflow of the loan at the beginning of the period and the repayment of the loan at the end of the period. You suspect that interest rates will go up. To hedge the company's exposure, you decide to enter into an agreement whereby a bank pays the company the amount of its interest costs, regardless of how much they fluctuate (shown on the third line). In return, the company agrees to pay the bank a fixed interest amount for the life of the agreement (shown in the last line). On a net basis, the floating payments cancel out, and the company is left paying a fixed rate of interest. It transformed its exposure from floating rate, where you were concerned with fluctuating cash flows, to a fixed rate, where your only concern is that the company might end up paying a high rate of interest if rates fell. It swapped its floating rate for a fixed rate.

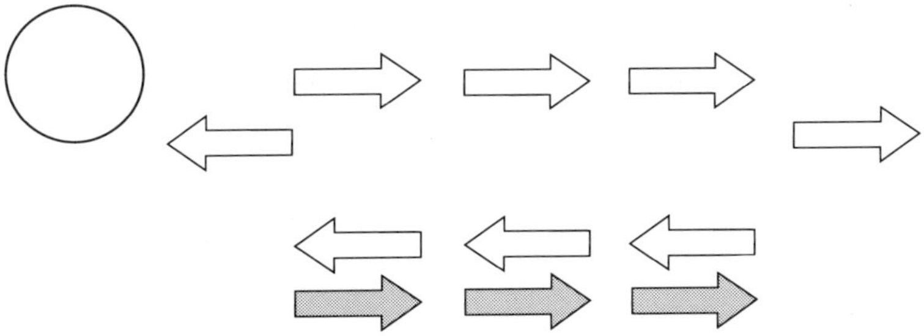

Illustration 4.3 Swap

With a swap, one side agrees to make payments on the basis of an interest rate that will not change over the period. The other side agrees to make payments on the basis of an interest rate that changes periodically, usually every one, three, or six months. If you compare a swap to an FRA (see Illustrations 4.1 and 4.3), you will see that the swap is a series of FRA transactions strung together.

For example, a company enters into a two-year swap with a bank on an amount of $50 million. It agrees to pay the bank 8 percent per annum every three months. The bank agrees to pay the company the average prime rate during each three-month interval. The swap is a symmetric hedge in that the company pays 8 percent whether prime is 5 percent or 10 percent.

The company and the derivatives bank do not exchange principal payments, only interest payments. In fact, only the net of the two interest payments is exchanged. Also, the swap has absolutely no effect on the company's obligation to repay the money borrowed to the lending bank.

CAPS

A *cap* is an agreement that sets an upper limit on the interest rate a company will pay, but allows the company to enjoy the benefit of lower rates. The company can choose the upper limit it desires.

Illustration 4.4 shows how the cap operates. White arrows represent floating rates. Gray arrows represent the cap. The vertical distance from the arrow to the base line indicates the level of the rate. Each time an interest rate is reset, the company has the choice of either paying the market rate or paying the cap rate. As such, it is an asymmetric hedge. Clearly a borrower will choose the lower of the two.

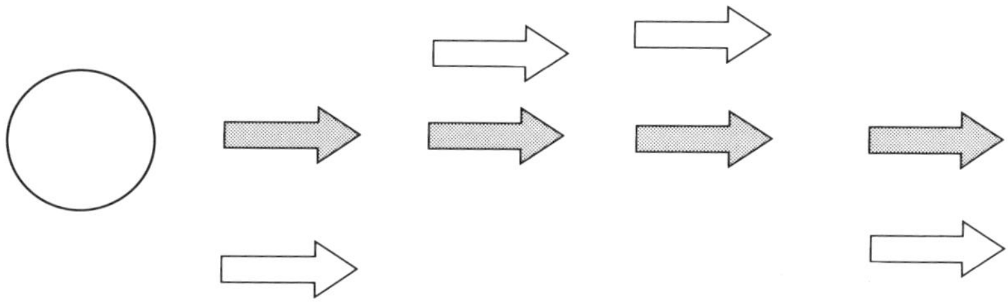

Illustration 4.4 Cap

The buyer of the cap pays a premium for the right to choose the rate it pays. For example, your company buys a 6-percent cap on three-month Libor (London interbank offered rate) for one year on $75 million.[2] You pay the bank a 0.60 percent premium on that amount two days after the agreement is made. You are protecting the company from increases in interest rates when loan rates are reset three, six, and nine months hence.

Let's look at what happens when it is time to pay interest on the loan and settle the cap contract. If interest rates have risen to 7 percent as feared:

You paid:	0.60%	premium
You pay:	7.00%	on the one-year loan
You receive:	1.00%	from cap agreement (7% minus 6% cap)
Your net rate:	**6.60%**	

If interest rates subsequently fall to 5 percent:

You paid:	0.60%	premium
You pay:	5.00%	on the one-year loan
You receive:	0%	from cap agreement
Your net rate:	**5.60%**	

FLOORS

Floors do for investors what caps do for borrowers. They provide insurance against an unfavorable movement in rates. For borrowers, it is a rise in rates; for investors, it is a fall in rates. Just as with insurance policies, investors pay a premium and choose the level at which they want the protection to become effective.

Your company is investing excess funds in commercial paper and is subject to monthly rate changes. To protect against a fall in rates, you buy a floor. Specifically, you buy a 5-percent floor on $200 million for one year with one month commercial paper as the reference rate. The bank charges a premium of 0.50 percent on $200 million. It is a flat fee payable two days after the transaction is agreed upon. Illustration 4.5 is similar to that used for the cap. White arrows represent the interest flows on commercial paper; gray arrows represent the floor. The vertical distance from the base line represents the level of rates.

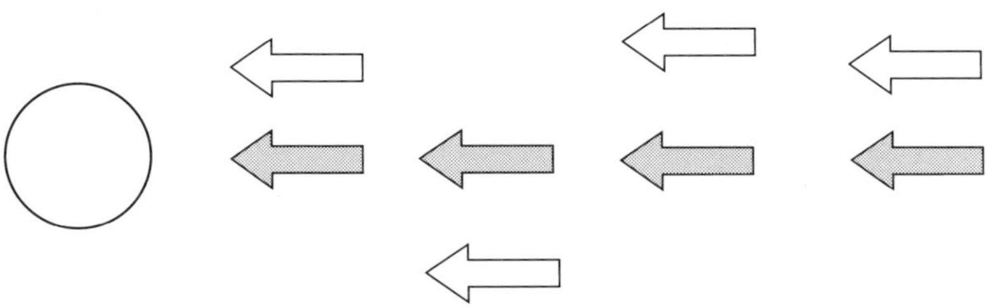

Illustration 4.5 Floors

Like caps, floors are an asymmetric hedge. You enjoy the benefit of rates above the 5-percent level, and are compensated if they go below 5 percent. If you are correct and commercial paper rates fall to 4 percent, the settlement of the investment and the floor are:

You paid:	0.50%	premium
You receive:	4.00%	from commercial paper investment
You receive:	1.00%	from floor agreement (5% minus 4%)
Your net rate:	**4.50%**	

A couple of months later rates rise to 6.0 percent. The settlement of the investment and the floor are:

You paid:	0.50%	premium
You receive:	6.00%	from commercial paper investment
You receive:	0%	from floor agreement
Your net rate:	**5.50%**	

NONMARKET ALTERNATIVES

Companies should consider a number of alternatives outside the market-oriented alternatives discussed in this book. Some can provide more permanent solutions to exposure situations than market alternatives.

MATCH EXPOSURE

A company matches an exposure by creating—in the opposite direction—cash flows of the same amount and same reset characteristics. A company holding surplus cash should look at the exposures on its liability side when it invests. If you work for a finance company or have finance company subsidiaries, a natural hedge might be easiest for you. For example, you can offset your floating rate borrowing exposures with short term investments. Compare the costs of creating these natural hedges to derivatives solutions.

ISSUE EQUITY

Companies particularly sensitive to interest rate fluctuations should explore new equity as a substitute for funded debt.

ACCELERATE RECEIVABLES/LAG PAYABLES

These alternatives effectively lower the amount of debt a company is required to carry to support its operations. Examine the cost of lagging payables and whether that cost is sensitive to movements in interest rates. Similarly, accelerating receivables is a trade off between the sales side of the operation and the treasury. By definition, these actions reduce exposure to rising interest rates.

DETERMINE CORRELATION BETWEEN INTEREST RATES AND PRODUCT PRICES

A number of companies have found that as interest rates rise, their product prices rise and fall in tandem. This seems to hold true particularly for oil companies. As a result, many companies in this position do not hedge interest rate exposure. Product pricing naturally will cover it. The degree of correlation is particular to each industry, so you need to study how it applies to yours.

DO NOTHING

One of the most popular alternatives for addressing exposure is to do nothing. After having measured the possible consequences of the exposure and having looked at the alternatives and their costs, companies often reach the conclusion that the best course of action is to do nothing. An unfavorable rate movement may not be of any consequence to the company, or the cost and trouble of creating a hedge is disproportionate to the problem. Having made that decision once, however, is not a good reason for ignoring the situation in the future. A change in circumstances can turn a once small problem into one of major consequence.

NOTES

1. Classification suggested by Benton E. Gup and Robert Brooks, *Interest Rate Risk Management,* New York, Irwin Professional Publishing, 1993, Chapter 1.

2. The London interbank offered rate (Libor) is the most common rate index used in corporate banking. It is the rate index for the Eurodollar market.

CHAPTER 5

How to Choose a Hedge

In this chapter, we look at methods for choosing whether a swap, FRA, futures, or cap is the best hedge. To be a strong hedge, the derivative chosen should match the rate reset pattern of the exposure, and the index should move the same amount as the exposure for any movement in rates. Another test is to compare the change in the value of the hedge from a change in interest rates to the change in the value of the exposure from the same change in interest rates. In a strong hedge, the change in values is the same.

Making this determination is not a simple process. You do not know some of the facts when you have to make your choice. For example, you do not know what interest rates will be six months from now, or what the premium for a cap will be one year from now. So you need a framework for making the choice, one that pulls in all the available information.

Basically the framework looks at cost and earning elements for each alternative and makes the comparisons graphically and mathematically. Let's say your company is expanding operations in Italy and France. You are considering a number of alternatives including a

- bank loan
- public note issue
- bank loan and a swap
- bank loan and FRAs
- bank loan and futures
- bank loan and a cap

BANK LOAN

The terms of the loan from a bank syndicate are: $50 million, 5 years, principal payable at maturity, six-month Libor, lending spread of 1 percent. If you do nothing about this exposure, you will pay whatever the future six-month Libor rate is, plus the lending spread. One way of showing this exposure is a graph that compares possible future interest rates and the company's cost of funds. Illustration 5.1 shows that for each increase in interest rates in the future, the cost of funds goes up as much.

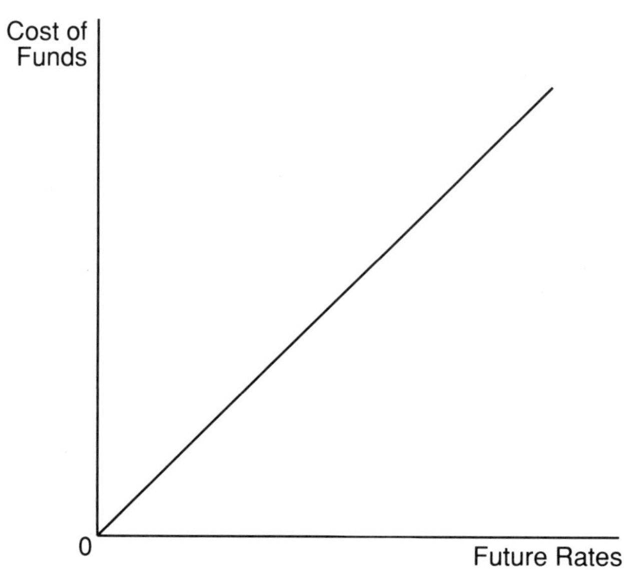

Illustration 5.1 Bank Loan

PUBLIC NOTE ISSUE

With this alternative, the company issues a five-year fixed rate note in the market to finance its expansion. This removes any question of fluctuating cash flows over the five-year period. The five-year note will be priced at the five-year Treasury rate plus the quality spread. A quality spread is the difference between the rate companies pay for funds and what the U.S. Treasury pays for the same maturities. Quality spreads are discussed more in Chapter 6. As with the previous alternative, the public note issue can be depicted graphically (see Illustration 5.2). Regardless of the course of interest rates, the cost of funds does not change.

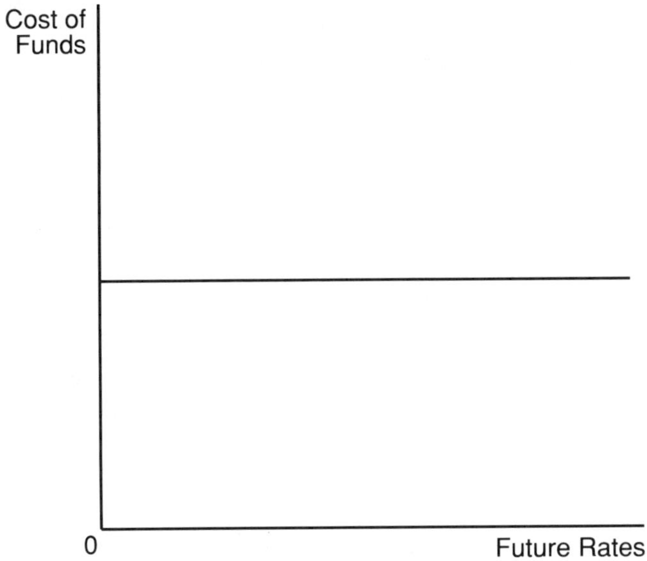

Illustration 5.2 Public Note Issue

SWAP

This alternative combines a bank loan with a swap to fix the interest payments for the life of the loan. The basis for pricing swaps is the U.S. Treasury yield curve plus a swap spread. During 1993 to 1995, swap spreads beyond two years ranged from 20 to 45 basis points. In return for paying a fixed rate, the derivatives bank pays the company Libor (see Illustration 5.3).

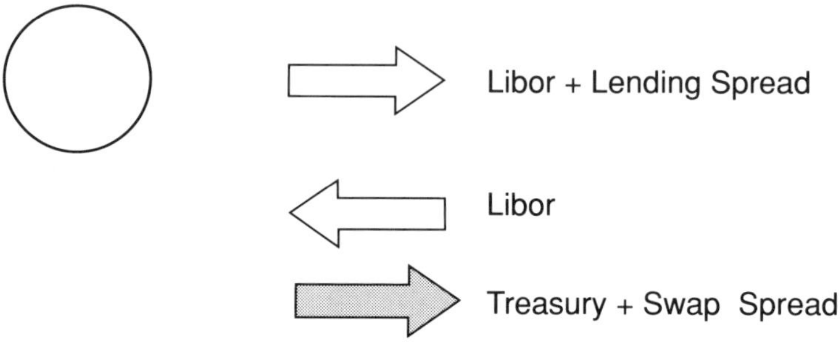

Illustration 5.3 Swap

The net result of the transaction is that the funding cost is the Treasury rate, plus the swap spread, plus the lending spread. The company pays and receives Libor, so these cost elements cancel one another out. The graphic representation of this alternative is the same as Illustration 5.2. Only the height of the horizontal line will be different.

FORWARD RATE AGREEMENT (FRA)

This alternative combines a bank loan with a series of FRAs to fix the interest payments for the life of the loan. The basis for pricing FRAs is the same as for pricing swaps—the U.S. Treasury yield curve plus a swap spread. The only difference between a swap and a series of FRAs is that with a swap one fixed rate, known today, prevails through its life; whereas with a series of FRAs, you have a series of different rates, set today, over the life of the loan (see Illustration 5.4).

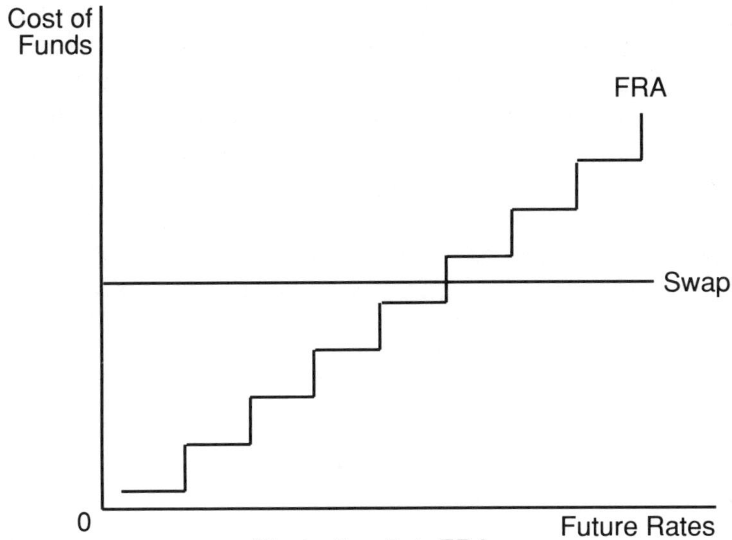

Illustration 5.4 FRA

The swap rate is the same as the average rate of a series of FRAs. Most companies would not enter into a series of FRAs to fix a rate for a longer term exposure; they would enter into a swap. However, having rates set today that rise over time may be advantageous. Cash is conserved at the start of a project; later in its life the project is better able to absorb interest expense. You may accomplish this with a customized swap as well as with a series of FRAs. (See Chapter 9, Step-Up and Step-Down Swaps and Caps.) In this chapter, we will treat a series of FRAs and a swap as the same financial instrument for the purpose of comparing it to other hedges.

FUTURES

As you recall from Chapter 4, futures have the same effect on exposure as FRAs and are priced similarly. Their principle difference is the flexibility in settlement; futures contracts have only four settlement days per year. Like FRAs, a series of futures could be used to hedge the company's floating rate loan. And like FRAs, futures produce a series of different rates, set today, over the life of the loan. However, futures generally will not be a strong hedge for a bank loan, because it is unlikely that interest rate reset dates will match.

CAP

This alternative combines a bank loan with a cap to insure that its interest costs do not go above a certain level. A premium is paid for this insurance. For comparison, we'll use the same rate for the cap as we used for the swap. In Chapter 9, we'll look at different cap levels, their advantages, and disadvantages.

With a cap in place, you would pay either Libor plus the lending spread or the cap rate plus the lending spread. In both cases, the premium cost needs to be added. In Illustration 5.5, the diagonal portion of the line shows that below the cap level your company's interest cost floats with market rates. The horizontal portion shows where the cap takes effect and you pay a fixed rate. The premium is reflected by the vertical distance between zero and where the diagonal line starts.

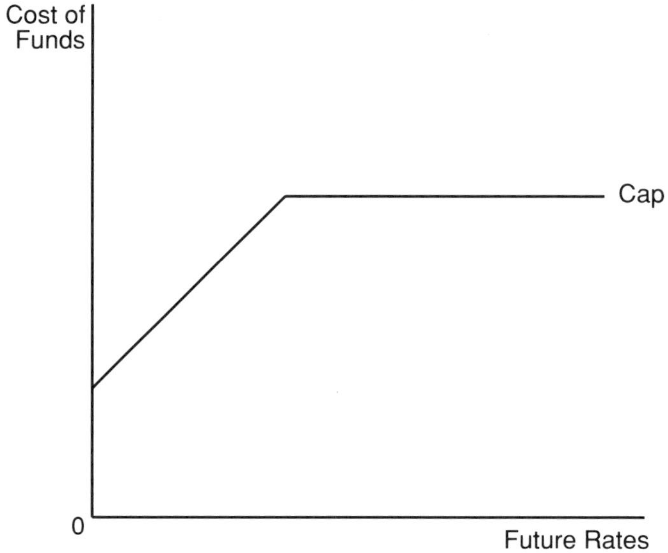

Illustration 5.5 Cap

COMPARISON OF ALTERNATIVES

Now let's compare the cost and earnings elements of each alternative in graphic and mathematical form. Illustration 5.6 brings together the alternatives in a single graph. Notice that the line for the cap is higher than the unhedged bank loan and higher than the swap rate. This distance reflects the premium paid for the cap.

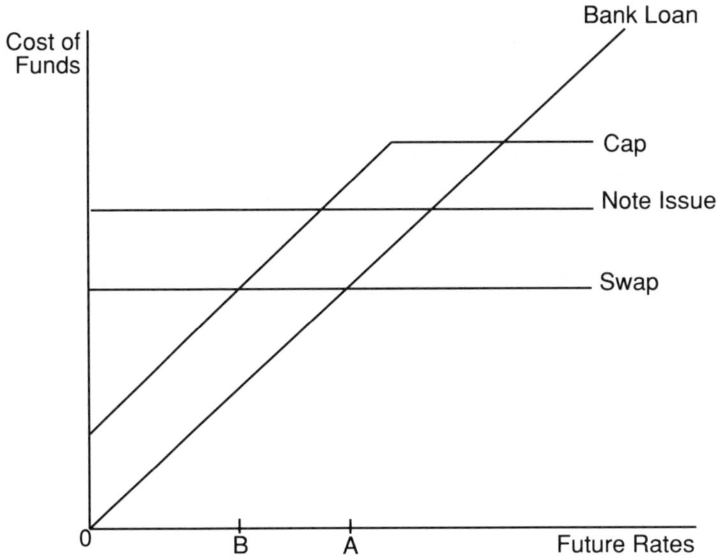

Illustration 5.6 Comparison of Alternatives

Based on the graph, we can make the following statements about the alternatives. A swap plus a bank loan is less expensive than a fixed rate public issue. If interest rates go no higher than point A on the graph, the best alternative is the bank loan and no hedge. If interest rates go higher than point A, the best alternative is the bank loan plus a swap. If rates go no higher than point B, a cap is better than a swap. The same set of choices can be expressed mathematically:

Assume:	Loan Spread (LS) = 1%
	Quality Spread (QS) = 1.5%
	Swap Spread (SS) = 0.3%
	Cap Premium (P) = 0.4% per annum
	Treasury (T) = 6%
	Libor (L) is variable

Loan:	L + LS	=	L + 1%
Note:	T + QS	=	6% + 1.5% = 7.5%
Swap:	T + SS + LS	=	6% + 0.3% + 1% = 7.3%
Cap:	T + SS + LS + P	=	6% + 0.3% + 1% + 0.4% = 7.7%
	or		
	L + LS + P	=	L + 1% + 0.4% = L + 1.4%

Comparing the swap and note issue:
If (SS + LS) is less than QS, the swap is less expensive.

Comparing the bank loan and the swap:
As long as L is less than T + SS, the unhedged bank loan is less expensive; above that, the swap plus the bank loan is preferable. Point A, in Illustration 5.6, is where L + LS = T + SS + LS. We know L + 1% = 7.3%; therefore point A is 6.3%. When Libor exceeds 6.3%, a swap is preferable.

Comparing the swap and the cap:
With the cap, the company would pay either:
(a) floating, L + LS + P, or
(b) fixed, T + SS + LS + P
depending on where rates are.

Comparing the floating portion to a swap:

Cap		**Swap**
L + LS + P	=	T + SS + LS
L + 1.4%	=	7.3%

If Libor is less than 5.9 percent, a cap is preferable to a swap. If Libor is greater than 5.9 percent, a swap is preferable to a cap. In Illustration 5.6, 5.9 percent corresponds to point B.

Comparing the fixed portion to a swap:

Cap		**Swap**
T + SS + LS + P	=	T + SS + LS
7.7%	=	7.3%

A cap always will be more expensive than a swap when short term interest rates exceed the swap rate. The difference is the premium.

This analysis is somewhat unsatisfactory because it does not reach a definite conclusion about which alternative to chose. It depends on two factors: where you expect rates to be over the next five years and the need for cash flow certainty. Given the alternatives:

- If you were confident that short term rates would average over 6.3 percent for the next five years, you would chose a bank loan and swap.
- If you believed short term rates would average less than 5.9 percent a year for the next five years, but could not afford interest exposures to increase dramatically, you would chose a bank loan and a cap.
- If you were confident short term rates would stay below 6.3 percent for the next five years, you would not hedge the bank loan.

In subsequent chapters, we will expand the analysis of how to choose an alternative.

In summary, the procedure for comparing alternatives is as follows:

- Ascertain that the rate reset dates and the instrument of the hedge match the exposure.
- Check that changes in interest rates have the same effect on the value of the hedge as they do on the value of the exposure.
- Express the performance of each alternative in terms of changing market rates, either mathematically or graphically.
- Eliminate any alternatives that are clearly dominated by another; in our example, a bank loan and swap dominated the note issue.
- Determine the interest rates where the alternatives produce equivalent results—points A and B in the example.
- Define the company's expectations about the course of future rates.
- Determine the ability to afford fluctuations in interest expense.

QUALITATIVE CONSIDERATIONS

In addition to the numerical elements, you should consider a number of other factors, particularly if the numerical analysis is close. Among these factors are the following elements:

Credit Risk: The company is exposed to the risk on a swap, FRA, and cap that its counterparty does not perform. This is not the case with the unhedged loan, public issue, or the futures market.

Credit Capacity: The bank is exposed to the risk that the company does not perform. Companies that enter into swaps with banks use up some of their credit availability. Credit availability is not used up by caps and futures.

Liquidity: You will want to have the ability to reverse the hedge transactions if you develop another view of interest rates or business circumstances change. Retiring a note issue or bank loan takes time, including negotiations to replace the funding source. Futures can be unwound in an instant. Swaps, caps, and FRAs can be unwound or offset in minutes.

Flexibility: Derivative products sold by financial institutions have the greatest flexibility. They are termed "over the counter" (OTC) products, to distinguish them from products traded on an exchange, like futures. Because derivatives is the business of pricing cash flows, regular and irregular, most interest rate exposures can be hedged with OTC derivatives. Futures and other exchange-traded derivatives have standardized dates and amounts. They cannot be as closely tailored to individual situations. However, this standardization and the near absence of credit risk are the reasons for the liquidity of exchange-traded derivatives.

Understanding: How easy is it for you to explain to your boss what you have done? Clearly you will lean toward what you understand best, what has been done before in the company, what takes the least amount of explanation, and what the boss understands best.

Administration: What has to be done before the transaction can be executed? Is it set up already? Does it have to be set up from scratch? A cap is preceded by an agreement. A swap is preceded by an agreement and a credit allocation by the counterparty. A futures transaction is preceded by an agreement, executed more quickly than a swap agreement, and a margin account. Futures, however, have daily margin movements. A company's treasury operations must be able to handle this level of detail.

Monitoring: What has to be done after the transaction is executed? You need to value the transaction periodically. Because futures prices are available instantly, a valuation of your position takes less than a minute. By knowing treasury rates and swap spreads, you can approximate swap values. For accuracy, you need to use a model or call a derivatives dealer. Cap values are the least transparent, since the volatility number used to calculate the value of a cap is not directly observable and is not usually published. You have to ask derivatives dealers. It is a good practice to ask more than one dealer. In addition, it is vital that the people doing the valuations be independent of those conducing the transactions and obtain their information from sources outside the firm. Management should receive the valuation results from these people. These are added functions for the accounting group.

Tax and Accounting: Neither tax nor accounting regulations are straightforward regarding derivatives, but they affect the outcome. A tax and accounting analysis needs to be part of every decision.

SOURCE

For the section on Qualitative Considerations, The Globcom Group, Ltd., *Derivatives Engineering,* Chicago, Irwin Professional Publishing, 1995, pp. 27-28.

CHAPTER 6

The Yield Curve

This chapter provides the foundation for understanding how derivatives are priced. We'll look at the yield curve more closely than you usually do by looking at the zero-coupon curve, forward rates, and quality spreads. The zero-coupon curve is used to value cash flows, particularly those that are irregular or do not correspond to the pattern of standard financial securities. Forward rates are the basis for constructing hedges for exposures that start in the future. Quality spreads, one of the determinants of swap pricing, are one of the reasons for the existence of the swap market.

YIELD CURVE

The yield curve depicts the relationship between yield and the maturity of financial instruments of the same credit quality. The "benchmark" yield curve is the U.S. Treasury curve, because the Treasury issues the greatest number of bills, notes, and bonds for the largest number of dates. Considered to be the risk-free yield curve, the Treasury curve is the basis to which all other borrowers are compared.

As shown in Illustration 6.1, yield curves have different shapes. Typical shapes include a positive slope, flat, or negative slope. A positively sloped yield curve means that short term rates are lower than long term rates. A flat curve means they are the same. And a negatively sloped curve means that short term rates are higher than long term rates. It is not uncommon, however, to see a positive slope over the first few years of the yield curve and a negative slope thereafter. When rates are in flux, yield curves take on these mixed shapes.

The shape affects the price of a derivative and the willingness to hedge. When the yield curve is positively sloped, swaps and caps that cover exposure to rising rates will seem expensive in relation to today's rates.

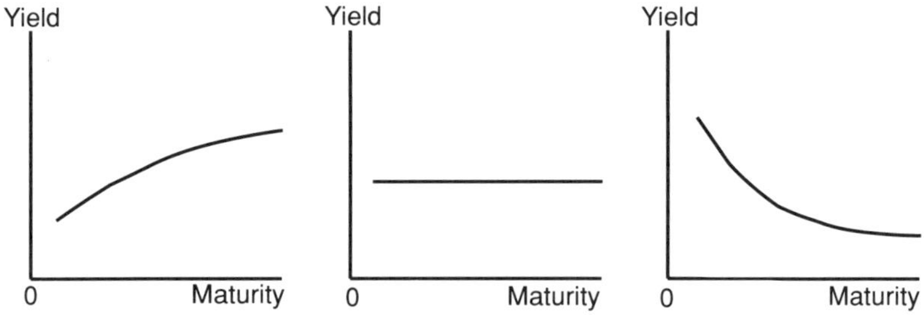

Illustration 6.1 Yield Curves

Three principle theories explain yield curves: expectations, liquidity preference, and market segmentation. The expectations theory, the most popular explanation of yield curve shape, says the yield curve is positively sloped when market participants expect rates to rise. In this situation, borrowers will borrow at a fixed rate for as long as possible, because money will only become more expensive. Investors will want to invest as short as possible, so that when rates rise, they will be able to use their maturing short term investments to buy assets that yield more. Therefore, little money is being invested in the long end of the market, but with a lot of demand. A lot of money is being invested in the short end, but with little demand. The expectations argument for a flat and negative slope curve follows the same logic.

The liquidity preference theory says that people want most of their money near at hand, as close to ready cash as possible. Therefore, they are most inclined to invest short term and need to be paid a premium to invest long term. According to this argument, the yield curve should be positively sloped most of the time.

Market segmentation theory argues that different investors and borrowers are active in different segments of the yield curve. For example, banks are the dominant short term investors and insurance companies are the dominant long term investors. Their particular appetites determine the level of rates in that segment of the curve and, as a result, the entire yield curve.

On their own, none of these theories are completely satisfactory. They do suggest, however, the number of variables that need to be considered when looking at the movement of interest rates. The important point is that when interest rates change, the change in three-month rates will be different from the change in five-year rates and both will be different from the change in 30-year rates.

ZERO-COUPON CURVE

The emphasis in this book is on cash flows that fluctuate due to changing interest rates. When you design hedges, you need to assign a value to future cash flows, where that value depends on interest rate levels. Then you can see how the values of the cash flows will be affected by changes in rate levels. The most common way of valuing future cash flows and putting them on a common basis is to calculate their present value. The present value formula is:

$$\text{Present Value} = \frac{\text{Cash Flow}}{(1 + R)^t}$$

where t = time
R = discount rate

There are two choices for the discount rate: a coupon bond that pays interest at stated intervals throughout its life, or a zero-coupon bond that pays all interest at maturity. The coupon bond is appropriate only for discounting a series of cash flows that match the pattern of that bond. For example, if you use a newly issued five-year note to value 10 semiannual cash flows, the result will be accurate. If you use the same five-year note to value 60 monthly cash flows, the result will be inaccurate. However, if you match up a series of cash flows with a series of zero-coupon bonds that mature on or near the cash flow dates, you obtain the correct result. Using zero-coupon rates is particularly important when the exposure cash flows are irregular.

The most appropriate way to value an exposure that consists of a series of cash flows is to value each flow. To do that, a zero-coupon curve is built. In practice, the zero-coupon yield curve is built from a rich set of coupon bond rates, as well as zero-coupon rates. Just as a yield curve contains the yield for various maturities, the zero-coupon curve contains zero-coupon rates for various maturities. Illustration 6.2 shows the relationship between a zero-coupon curve and a yield curve. When the yield curve is positively sloped, the zero curve will be above it. When the yield curve is negatively sloped, the zero curve will be below it.

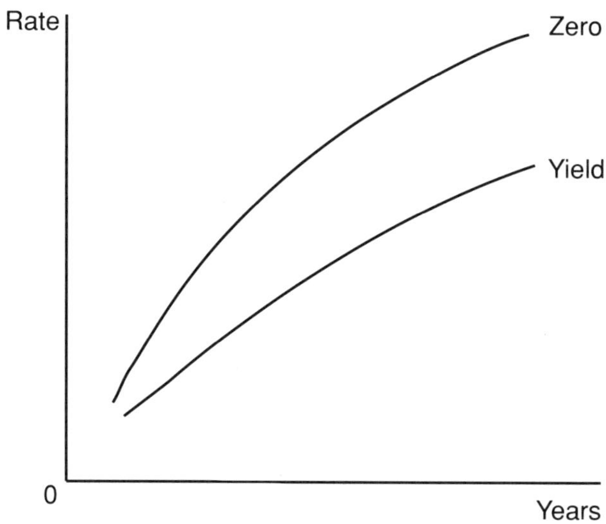

Illustration 6.2 Zero-Coupon Curve and Yield Curve

Derivative dealers use a zero-coupon curve to value cash flows, and they value each flow separately. This often leads to differences with people who apply a yield-to-maturity rate to an entire series of cash flows. A simple example will show the difference. Let's assume an exposure consists of a series of yearly interest payments of 10 percent on a four-year loan of $100 million. Zero-coupon rates for years one through four are 5 percent, 6 percent, 7 percent, and 8 percent. The yield to maturity for four years is 7.15 percent. The present value of the cash flows using the zero-coupon rates is $33,937,000. The present value of the cash flows using the yield-to-maturity rate is $33,758,000, a difference of $179,000. Only when the yield curve is flat will the two curves yield the same results. The steeper (positive or negative) the yield curve, the more the results will diverge.

FORWARD RATES

A forward rate is the interest rate that applies to a period in the future. To illustrate, let's look at a new situation. You know that in one month your company will receive its quarterly royalty fees from its subsidiary in Ireland. The money has been designated to purchase equipment three months later. During the interim period, you want to earn as much as possible on the surplus funds. The problem you face is that you see interest rates falling, and think that in one month the three-month investment rate may be as much as 1 percent lower than today.

You would like to lock in a rate today for the future period. You could invest money today for four months to take advantage of higher rates. And since the company does not have the money, it could borrow from the bank for one month and repay the loan when the royalties arrived. The net effect would be to invest money for three months, one month from today, at a rate fixed today. Illustration 6.3 shows the flow of funds.

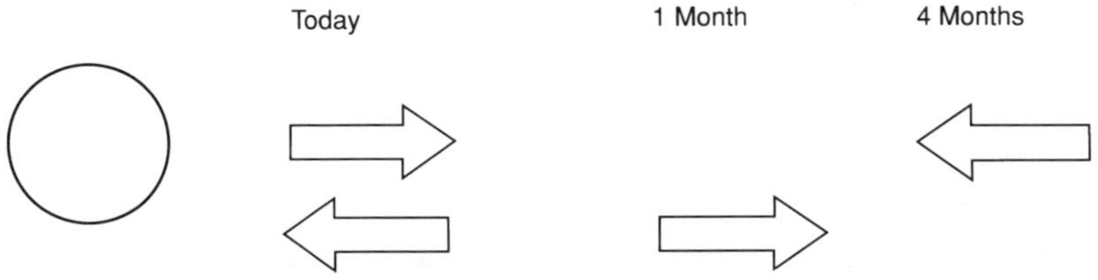

Illustration 6.3 Forward Rate, 3 Months

We'll develop the formula for calculating the forward rate in two steps. The first step looks only at rate levels. If the investment rate for four months is 6 percent, and the borrowing rate for one month is 5 percent, you have fixed a rate of 6.33 percent for the three-month investment. The forward investment rate for three months is higher than the four-month rate because the company was earning 6 percent on its investment, but borrowing at only 5 percent for the first month, a pick up of 1 percent for one month. The calculation is:

$$6.33\% = \frac{6\% \times 4 \text{ months} - 5\% \times 1 \text{ month}}{3 \text{ months}}$$

$$\text{rate} = \frac{\text{investment rate} \times \text{time} - \text{borrowing rate} \times \text{time}}{\text{net period of investment}}$$

The second step is to account for interim interest payments and receipts. The cash flows in Illustration 6.3 make it clear that there is interest expense in the first six months not recognized in the formula. This effectively lowers the forward rate for the investor a bit. The following formula recognizes these interim cash flows. The difference is in the second term of the denominator.

$$\text{Forward rate} = \frac{[R(i) \times \text{days}(i)] - [R(b) \times \text{days}(b)]}{[\text{days}(i) - \text{days}(b)] \times [1 + (R(b) \times \frac{\text{days}(b))]}{36{,}000}}$$

where:
- R(i) = investment rate
- days(i) = number of investment days
- R(b) = borrowing rate
- days(b) = number of borrowing days

To illustrate the formula, we will use the numbers from the previous example. You invested for four months at 6 percent and borrowed for one month at 5 percent. The more accurate forward rate is 6.31 percent, slightly less than the 6.33 percent calculated by the simplified version of the formula.

$$6.31\% = \frac{(6 \times 120) - (5 \times 30)}{(120 - 30) \times [1 + (5 \times \frac{30}{36{,}000})]}$$

This formula is designed to find a forward rate for an investor. For the borrower, simply substitute 'i' for 'b' and 'b' for 'i'. We developed this formula in a way that the logic was apparent. However, it is somewhat unwieldy and is not universally applicable.

A more general formula is :

$$\left[\frac{1 + (R(i) \times days(i)/360)}{1 + (R(b) \times days(b)/360} - 1\right] \times \frac{360}{days(i) - days(b)}$$

where: R(i) = investment rate
days(i) = number of investment days
R(b) = borrowing rate
days(b) = number of borrowing days

The calculation of the three-month borrowing rate is:

$$6.31\% = \left[\frac{1 + (.06 \times 120/360)}{1 + (.05 \times 30/360)} - 1\right] \times \frac{360}{90}$$

A forward rate is composed of two rates: the one starting today to the *end* of the transaction and the one starting today to the *beginning* of the transaction. When there is a positive yield curve, the forward rate will generally be higher than any of the rates used to calculate it. The example demonstrates this. When there is a negative yield curve, the forward rate will generally be lower than any of the rates used to calculate it. In locking in a borrowing or deposit rate for the future, you should compare the forward rate to what you are expecting interest rates will be at that time.

QUALITY SPREADS

Quality spreads describe the rate difference at which institutions of different credit standing borrow for each maturity on the yield curve. The reference point is the U.S. Treasury yield curve. Companies speak in terms of their ability to borrow at, say, 30 basis points "over the curve," meaning they are paying the five-year treasury rate of 6.50 percent plus 0.30 percent, or 6.80 percent. The reason for thinking about quality spreads in the context of derivatives is that they are an important factor in interest rate swap pricing. They describe the comparative advantage that companies have using the swap market, and they are used when you compare fixed and floating rate borrowing against other forms of hedging.

Quality spreads generally follow the bond rating of the company. The higher the rating, the lower the spread. For example, on a given day in the U.S. public debt market, the U.S. Treasury may borrow for 10 years at 7.15 percent, a company rated AAA would borrow at 7.55 percent, a company rated A would borrow at 7.90 percent, and a company rated BBB would borrow at 8.05 percent. The quality spread between the AAA company and the U.S. Treasury is 0.40 percent, also expressed as 40 basis points. Quality spreads change over time on the basis of the state of the economy, corporate profitability, the absolute level of interest rates, and the amount of money investors have available. For many of the same reasons, the differences between companies of different credit quality also changes.

Illustration 6.4 shows the evolution of quality spreads for 10-year issues over the last 4 years. Over this brief period, the borrowing advantage of an AAA company over a BBB company ranged from 40 to 100 basis points.

Illustration 6.4 Quality Spreads

Source: Data from Bloomberg, U.S. *Fair Value Sector*, IN02, IN05, IN10, IN30, H15T2, H15T3, H15T10, H15T30, August 2, 1995.

Another way to look at quality spreads is to compare them across maturities, from short term to long term. Illustration 6.5 shows the average over the last four years. If you are a lower rated company, the cost of borrowing longer rises more steeply for you than for an AAA company.

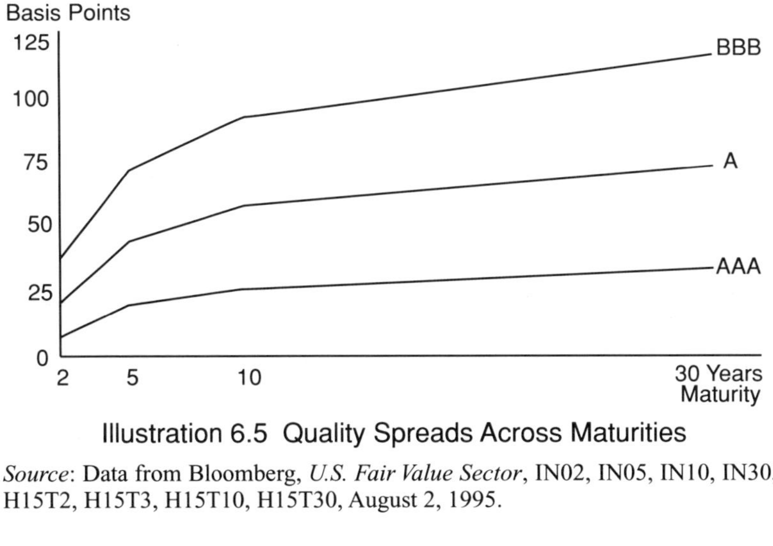

Illustration 6.5 Quality Spreads Across Maturities

Source: Data from Bloomberg, *U.S. Fair Value Sector*, IN02, IN05, IN10, IN30, H15T2, H15T3, H15T10, H15T30, August 2, 1995.

CHAPTER 7

How to Execute FRAs and Futures

In previous chapters, we looked at FRAs and futures on a conceptual level. This chapter, with more detail about these derivatives, will concentrate on the information needed to execute a transaction. The next three chapters are about how basic derivatives products work.

To illustrate the details of FRAs and futures, let's say your company intends to borrow $77 million for six months on May 12, which is three months from now. The rate will be set at the prevailing six-month Libor rate plus a lending spread. You want to hedge the exposure today to rising interest rates. Your two alternatives are FRAs and futures. The futures contracts used is the Eurodollar contract, because it most closely matches the company's borrowing index. This contract represents three-month Eurodollar deposits. Eurodollar futures contracts are shown on June 19 and September 18 because they settle on four specified dates each year. Illustration 7.1 shows the flows of the two alternatives.

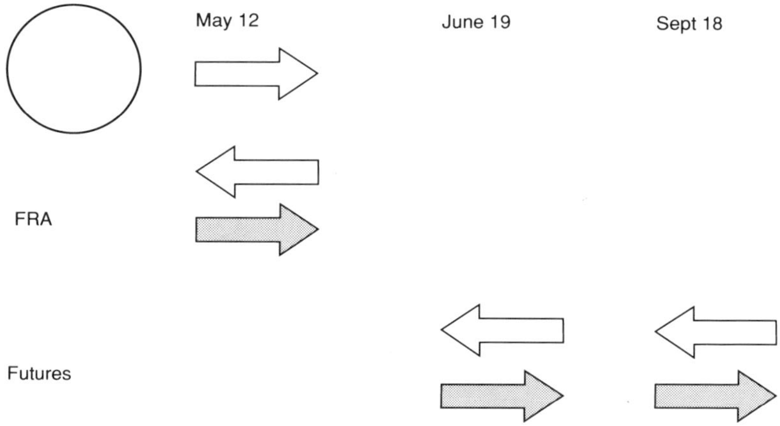

Illustration 7.1 FRA and Futures Contracts

CONFIRMATIONS

To explain these derivatives, we are going to follow the details of confirmations exchanged between a bank and a company after a transaction. We will identify the important aspects of the transactions.

FORWARD RATE AGREEMENTS

The details of the FRA confirmation are:

Notional Amount:	$77 million
Trade Date:	February 10
FRA Buyer (Fixed Rate Payer):	Company
FRA Seller (Floating Rate Payer):	Bank
Value Date:	May 12
Fixed Rate:	6.42%
Floating Rate Option:	Six-month Libor, Telerate page 3750
Floating Rate Day Count Fraction:	Actual/360
FRA Discounting:	Applicable

The translation of the FRA contract is:

Buyer: The market terminology is to "buy" or "sell" an FRA. Buying an FRA protects a borrower from a rise in rates. Selling an FRA protects an investor from a fall in rates. This convention becomes clearer when you think about what happens when the contract is settled on May 12. If the rate for that day were 7 percent, you would receive the difference between 7 percent and 6.42 percent. You bought an FRA at one rate and sold at a higher rate. This earning offsets the interest cost of 7 percent (plus lending spread) that you will pay on the loan.

If the rate for that day were 6 percent, you pay the bank the difference between 6.42 percent and 6 percent. You bought at one rate and sold at a lower rate. This payment increases the interest cost of 6 percent (plus lending spread) that you will pay on the loan.

Value Date: The value date is the date the money moves. The convention in the Eurodollar market is to set rates two business days ahead of the value date. On May 10, the bank will look at the six-month Libor rate. The rate on that day is for loans that start on May 12.

Fixed Rate: This is the rate on the FRA that is priced by the bank. It becomes the fixed rate for the company's six-month loan, plus the lending spread.

Floating Rate Option: This is the index rate against which the FRA rate will be compared. On May 10, the bank will look at six-month Libor value for May 12 and compare it to the fixed rate.

Telerate 3750: Telerate is a rate service. Page 3750 lists Libor rates for all maturities up to one year as of 11 a.m. London time. It is a standard reference for FRAs and swaps.

Floating Rate Day Count Fraction: This is the method for calculating interest. (See Cahpter 8 for greater detail.)

FRA Discounting: The payoff on an FRA is generally discounted by the floating rate using the floating rate day count convention.

FUTURES

Details of the futures contracts:

The company *sells 77 June* Eurodollar contracts at 93.55 and sells *77 September Eurodollar contracts* at 93.50. It posts *margin* with the Exchange of approximately 0.061 percent of the face amount of the contracts, which is $93,940.

Translation of the futures transaction:

93.55 and 93.50: The convention in the Eurodollar futures market is to quote prices. The yield is 100 minus the price, for example, 100 – 93.50 = 6.50 percent. When interest rates rise, futures prices go down. When interest rates fall, futures prices go up.

Sells: The market terminology is to sell and buy futures contracts. Selling a futures contract protects a borrower from a rise in rates. Buying a futures contract protects an investor from a fall in rates. The buying and selling convention is the reverse of an FRA, because FRAs are quoted in terms of rates and futures are quoted in terms of prices. The convention of selling a futures contract to protect against a rise in rates becomes clearer when we look at what happens at settlement.

You have sold futures contracts at 93.50; if interest rates rose, the futures contract price could move to 93.00. You can then buy back the same contracts you sold but at a lower price. The earnings will compensate the company for borrowing at a higher rate.

June, September: Eurodollar futures contracts settle on the third Wednesday of March, June, September, and December. The June and September contracts are the closest to the company's exposure in mid-May.

Eurodollar Futures Contract: This contract is dealt at the Chicago Mercantile Exchange. It represents three-month Eurodollar deposits in an amount of $1,000,000. A change in one basis point, from 93.01 to 93.00, is equal to $25 on the $1,000,000 contract. Forty contracts, extending out 10 years, are traded on the Exchange. Table 7.1 shows the transcription of a Eurodollar futures screen printout from Reuters. The prices are also found daily in the *The Wall Street Journal*.

77 June and 77 September: Because Eurodollar futures contracts represent three-month money, it is necessary to put two contracts together to create a hedge for a six-month loan.

Margin: The Chicago Mercantile Exchange, as do all futures and options exchanges, requires buyers and sellers to post margin. The margin insures that any losses on the contracts can be made up from the available pool of funds.

Hedge Level: You sold contracts at 93.55 and 93.50. This translates into a hedge level of 6.53 percent.[1] The rate is higher than the

Table 7.1 Eurodollar Futures Prices

SEP5*	94.17	MAR9	93.46
DEC5	94.32	JUN9	93.40
MAR6	94.41	SEP9	93.35
JUN6	94.33	DEC9	93.26
SEP6	94.24	MAR0	93.25
DEC6	94.08	JUN0	93.19
MAR7	94.03	SEP0	93.12
JUN7	93.92	DEC0	93.03
SEP7	93.85	MAR1	93.03
DEC7	93.73	JUN1	92.97
MAR8	93.71	SEP1	92.92
JUN8	93.64	DEC1	92.83
SEP8	93.57	MAR2	92.82
DEC8	93.47	JUN2	92.80

*SEP5 refers to the contract that settles on the third Wednesday of September 1995.

FRA because it starts about five weeks after the exposure, and theyield curve is positively sloped. (This is observed from the futures prices. The price for June 1996 is higher than the price for September 1996, meaning that the rate for June is lower than the rate for September.)

SETTLEMENT

As part of your analysis of the alternatives, you would test the FRA and futures to determine how good the protection from each alternative would be if interest rates went up. To test the robustness of the hedges, we'll assume that six-month Libor goes up to 7 percent on May 10.

FORWARD RATE AGREEMENTS

We have represented the FRA as having fixed and floating legs. The fixed leg is 6.42 percent, the floating leg is 7 percent. Rather than the bank making a payment of 7 percent on $77 million and the company making a payment of 6.42 percent on $77 million, the payments are netted and the net amount is paid. On May 12, the bank pays you the difference between the two rates. Because the difference is paid at the beginning of the period rather than at the end of six months, the amount is discounted. The formula for determining the payment follows. (The numerator is the formula for an amount of interest; the denominator is the discount factor.)

$$\frac{\text{Amount} \times (\text{Floating rate} - \text{Fixed rate}) \times \text{days} / 360}{1 + (\text{Floating rate} \times \text{days} / 360)}$$

where the floating rate is that observed on May 10.

You receive $216,907 from the bank:

$$\frac{77{,}000{,}000 \times (0.07 - 0.0642) \times 181/ 360}{1 + (0.07 \times 181 / 360)}$$

To ensure that your borrowing cost on the total amount is no greater than 6.42 percent, you will reduce the amount the company borrows by $216,907.

FUTURES

Settlements are made between the date the futures were initially sold and May 10. Each day, the Chicago Mercantile Exchange looks at the closing prices on the contracts you sold and compares those prices to the closing prices on the Exchange that day. If the closing price is higher than the one at which you sold, the Exchange will request additional margin. If the price rises again the next day, more margin will be requested. If the price goes down on the third day, margin will be released. If you decide to hedge exposures with futures, you will require strong operational capability to monitor the flow of funds in and out of the margin account.

On May 10, you buy back the 154 contracts you sold. You do not wait until the contracts settle in June and September because you want to capture the current values. Because we assumed interest rates rose, the prices of the futures contracts are down. The June contract falls to 93.05 from 93.55, and the September contract falls to 93.00 from 93.50. This means you buy back the contracts at a gain. The money is wired to the company's account the day after. The gain is calculated as:

(Sales price − Purchase price) × number of contracts × $25
The gain on the 77 June contracts is $96,250.
(93.55 – 93.05) × 77 × $25
The gain on the 77 September contracts is $96,250.
(93.50 – 93.00) × 77 × 25

The total gain of $192,500 falls about $25,000 short of compensating the company for the increase in interest rates. Two factors contribute to the shortfall: first, it was not possible to match the futures market dates to the borrowing date; second, Eurodollar futures prices do not necessarily move as much as Eurodollar interest rates. The June and September contracts move only 50 basis points, whereas the rate at which the company borrows moves 58 basis points from the FRA rate it locks in. These two elements are termed *basis risk*. The basis risk of futures contracts is one of the reasons many companies favor OTC products, such as FRAs.

EXECUTING THE FRA CONTRACT

You buy an FRA because it provides a more tailored fit to the company's exposure. Before the company can execute an FRA transaction, however, it must have credit availability from its bankers. Moreover, you should have read the standard documentation for FRAs (see Chapter 12). The company can approximate the rate by checking futures prices in the newspaper or by getting an indication level from its banker. You compare the indicated rate to your expectations of where rates will be in the future and decide to hedge none, part, or all of the company's exposure. You call two banks at the same time and specify the

- company is a buyer of an FRA
- starting date
- period to be covered
- amount

In our example, the starting date is May 12, the period to be covered is six months, and the amount is $77,000,000. Confirmation should arrive no later than 24 hours after the transaction. (This is a small but important point because it tells you about the accuracy and efficiency of the bank's back room operations.)

After a bank sells you an FRA, it has an interest rate exposure. The bank's first response is to hedge the exposure with futures. The bank will then manage the mismatch between the terms of the FRA and the futures contracts until it is able to find an FRA that provides a more precise offset.

SUMMARY OF CHARACTERISTICS

Table 7.2 sums up the similarities and differences between FRAs and Eurodollar futures. It is a useful way of setting up your options.

Table 7.2 Summary of Characteristics of FRAs and Futures

Characteristics	FRAs	Eurodollar Futures
Size of contract	Variable	$1,000,000
Transaction amounts	Over $1 billion	Over $1 billion
Dates	Variable	Four days a year
Periods	Variable	Three months
Price specification	Rate (%)	Price (93.87)
Basis risk	No	Often
Payoff determination	Contract rate vesus verus reference rate	Old contract price versus new contract price
Payoff timing	Up front, discounted	Daily
Settlement	Cash	Cash
Credit risk for company	Banks, various ratings	Exchange, AAA rated
Credit extended to company	Bank credit	None, margin is posted by the company daily

PRICING

As described in Chapter 6, FRAs and futures are forward rates. The same elements and formulas are used to derive their prices. An FRA rate for three months that settles on the same date as a Eurodollar futures contract will be the same. The FRA rate will be expressed as 6.24 percent; the futures price will be expressed as 93.76. If the two rates are not the same, professional dealers will buy the underpriced contract and sell the overpriced one until they are the same.

NOTE

1. The rate of 6.53 percent derived from the futures contracts was done as follows:

   Convert prices to rates, in decimal form.

   $100 - 93.55 = 0.0645$ and $100 - 93.50 = 0.0650$

   Compound the rates.

   Annualize to a full year—multiply by 360/182 since this is a six-month period.

   $$6.53 = \left\{ \left[1 + \left(0.0645 \times \frac{91}{360}\right) \right] \text{x} \left[1 + \left(0.065 \times \frac{91}{360}\right) \right] - 1 \right\} \times 360/182$$

   The generalized formula for putting together a number of futures contracts to generate a single period rate is:

   $$R = \left\{ \left[1 + \left(F(i) \times \frac{d(i)}{360}\right) \times 1 + \left(L \times \frac{d(L)}{360}\right) \right] - 1 \right\} \times 360/d\,(T)$$

   where:

   R = Eurodollar strip rate stated as an annualized money market yield

   L = Libor rate from the start date until the first futures contract date

   F(i) = futures contract rate expressed as (100 – 9x.xx)

   d(i) = actual number of days in each period

d(L) = number of days from the start date until the first futures contract date

d(T) = total number of days

The formula can be used to obtain a single rate for one year, starting January 10, 1996. The futures prices (and rates) for the four contracts starting March 20, 1996, are:

March	94.26	5.74%
June	94.11	5.89%
September	93.95	6.05%
December	93.74	6.26%

The Eurodollar deposit rate for the period from January 10 to March 20 is 5.57 percent.

The one year rate, R = 5.99%

$$\left[\left(1 + 0.0574 \times \frac{91}{360}\right) \times \left(1 + 0.0589 \times \frac{91}{360}\right) \times \left(1 + 0.0605 \times \frac{91}{360}\right)\right.$$

$$\left.\times \left(1 + 0.0626 \times \frac{22}{360}\right) \times \left(1 + 0.055 \times \frac{70}{360}\right) - 1\right] \times 360/365$$

CHAPTER 8

How to Execute Swap Transactions

Swaps are popular because they allow companies to create a different risk profile without changing the structure of their business. The use of swaps by corporations, financial institutions, and money managers is responsible for the explosion of the derivatives market. In 1989 about $500 billion in swap transactions took place. In 1994 the amount was nearly $6.2 trillion.[1]

Most nonfinancial alternatives (mentioned in Chapter 4) affect customers, suppliers, or stockholders. Companies are reluctant to do anything that affects its relations with outside parties when dealing with financial issues, so swaps are the preferred alternative. If you borrow at floating rates, swaps allow you to trade the risk of higher and variable interest payments for certainty. Often, you start out paying a higher rate for this certainty.

Another reason for the popularity of swaps is that most companies, from AAA to BBB, have found that swaps give them an economic advantage in financing. To illustrate, let's look at two companies. One is rated AAA and the other is rated BBB. The AAA company wants to increase the percentage of floating rate debt on its balance sheet. It considers increasing the size of its commercial paper program. Its commercial paper rate is equivalent to Libor minus five basis points. The alternative is to issue a five-year fixed rate note at treasuries plus 30 basis points and enter into a swap to convert the fixed rate note to a floating rate.

The BBB company wants to expand its plant and finance it with fixed rate debt. It considers issuing a five-year note at treasuries plus 110 basis points. Or it could borrow from its bank at Libor plus 50 basis points and enter into a swap to convert the floating rate to a fixed rate. Even though the AAA company can borrow in both the fixed and floating rate markets at better rates than the BBB company, it pays for the two companies to consider a trade with one another.

If the difference between the short term and long term rates at which the BBB company can borrow is not the same as the difference between short and long term rates at which the AAA company can borrow, a trade will be beneficial. Stated differently, if the companies' individual quality curves are not parallel, they should trade. The AAA company could issue the fixed rate note and the BBB company could borrow from the bank, just the opposite of the way they want to end up, *and then* exchange interest flows. Illustration 8.1 shows that if the swap spread is 45 basis points, both companies can achieve their objectives more cheaply by using a swap.

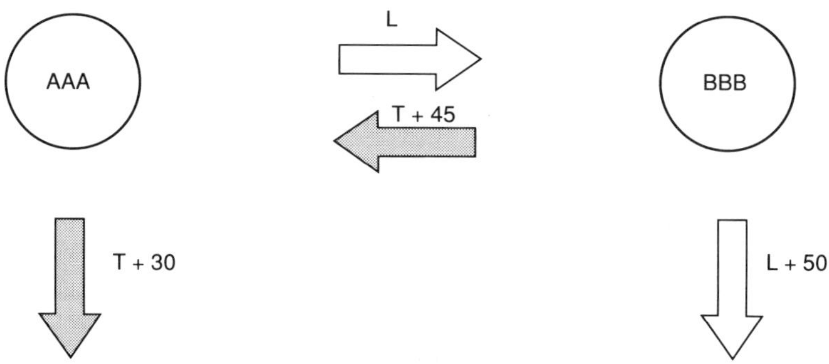

Illustration 8.1 Comparative Advantage of a Swap

Cash flows for the AAA company are:

Note issue	– (T + 30 basis points)
Swap (receive fixed)	+ (T + 45)
Swap (pay floating)	– L
Net floating rate cost	– (L – 15 basis points), compared to commercial paper program of Libor minus 5 basis points. On an amount of $50,000,000, this is worth $50,000 a year for five years.

Cash flows for the BBB company are:

Bank loan	– (L + 50 basis points)
Swap (pay fixed)	– (T + 45)
Swap (receive floating)	+ L
Net fixed rate cost	– (T + 95 basis points), compared to note issuance of treasuries plus 110 basis points. On a loan of $50,000,000, the savings is worth $75,000 a year for five years.

The companies could handle the arrangements for this swap themselves. But usually a commercial or investment bank is in the middle of the transaction because it performs two critical roles: credit intermediary and dealer. Both sides of the swap expect the other to perform for the next five years, so someone must evaluate their ability to make the payments. Banks are better equipped to make this evaluation than corporations. For that reason, a bank stands in the middle of the transaction and takes the risk of both companies; both companies take the risk of a bank.

In addition to the credit function, banks that act as swap dealers stand ready to enter into a transaction regardless of whether or not there is another company to offset the trade. As you can imagine, you seldom have two companies wanting to do a transaction for the same amount and the same time maturity—in the opposite direction. The bank manages the swap until another company is found.

In this chapter, we'll look at how to enter into a swap transaction. We will look at the details of swap transactions, examine the factors that affect swap pricing, and decide whether, as a borrower or investor, it is worthwhile to move from a lower floating rate to a higher fixed rate.

SWAP TRANSACTION

The details of the swap transaction the BBB company is considering are:

Notional Amount:	$50,000,000
Trade Date:	April 22, 1996
Effective Date:	April 24, 1996
Termination Date:	April 24, 2001
Fixed Rate Payer:	BBB Company
Fixed Rate:	8.00%
Fixed Rate Payer Payment Dates:	October 24, April 24
Fixed Rate Day Count Fraction:	30/360
Floating Rate Payer:	Bank
Floating Rate Payer Payment Dates:	October 24, April 24
First Floating Rate:	6.75%
Floating Rate Option:	6 month Libor, Reuters LIBO
Floating Rate Day Count Fraction:	Actual/360
Business Day Convention:	Modified following business day

When deciding to execute a swap transaction, you should specify all of these details to the banks quoting on the transaction. The dates, day count fractions, floating rate option, and business day convention should match as closely as possible the exposure being hedged. As you will see in the following discussion, details make a difference.

Notional Amount: This is the amount of the swap transaction (principal) on which interest payments are calculated. It is termed "notional" because principal amounts of the swap do not change hands.

Effective Date: The effective date is normally two business days from the date on which the transaction is entered into. On that date, interest starts to accrue on both the fixed rate leg and the floating rate leg of the swap.

First Floating Rate: For swaps that start two days from the trade date, the first floating rate is set at the same time as the fixed rate. It is the current market rate.

Floating Rate Option: The floating rate for any swap is based on an index that is public. In addition to Libor, common indices for corporate transactions are prime and commercial paper. Choose the rate index that most closely corresponds to the index governing your exposure.

Reuters LIBO: Reuters is a rate service and LIBO is a page number. Along with Telerate page 3750, they are the standard sources for the Libor index. The standard source for the prime and commercial paper indices is the Federal Reserve's H.15 Report, *Selected Interest Rates*.

Rate Day Count Fraction: This is derivatives terminology for the accrual method used to calculate interest. When a company borrows or invests, interest is calculated according to an accrual method. That's the fraction at the end of the formula that says how many days are in an interest period and how many days are in a year. The company's objective should be to match the method used for the exposure with the method used for the swap. The accrual method used affects the amount of interest paid. Two interest rates cannot be compared unless they are on the same accrual method. Table 8.1 shows the standard accrual methods, comments on their usage, and shows the different rates that generate the same amount of interest.

Table 8.1 Accrual Methods

Accural Method	Comment	Interest Rate that Generates the Same Interest Amount (%)
Actual/360	The numerator is the actual number of days in the interest calculation period. Used for calculating payments based on Libor.	8
Actual/365	Sometimes used for calculating payments on the fixed leg of the swap.	8.11*
Actual/Actual	Very similar to Actual/365, but in a Leap Year, 366 is used in the denominator.	8.13
30/360	Each month has 30 days, regardless of the actual count. The most common accural method for calculating payments on the fixed leg of the swap.	8.11*

* Over the course of a non-leap year, these methods would produce the same result. For a shorter period, the Actual/365 method will usually generate a larger interest payment.

Payment Dates: The three things to know about payments are: when they are made, how they are made, and the relation between when rates are set and when payments are made. The basic conventions for *when* payments are made are annually, semiannually, quarterly, or monthly. A swap that pays interest monthly is more valuable than one that pays annually, because it is better to have money now than later. Table 8.2 shows the affect of cash flow frequency for a swap with a fixed rate of 8 percent, paid annually. You would receive equivalent value if you were paid 7.85 percent semiannually, or 7.72 percent monthly.

Table 8.2 Payment Frequency and Interest Rates

Payment Frequency	Effective Interest Rate (%)
Annually	8
Semiannually	7.85
Quarterly	7.77
Monthly	7.72

The formula for converting an annual rate to a semiannual rate is:

$$S = 2 \times [(1 + A)^{\wedge}.5 - 1]$$

where: S = semiannual rate
A = annual rate

The formula for converting a semiannual rate to a monthly rate is:

$$M = 12 \times [(1 + S/2)^{\wedge}.166 - 1]$$

where: M = monthly rate

Like FRAs, payments on swaps are made on a net basis. The amount of interest owed on the fixed leg of the swap is calculated, the amount of interest owed on the floating leg of the swap is calculated, and the difference is paid to the appropriate party. For example, look at the payment after the first six months of the swap.

Company pays fixed: $\$50{,}000{,}000 \times 0.08 \times \frac{180}{360} = \$2{,}000{,}000$

Bank pays floating: $\$50{,}000{,}000 \times 0.0675 \times \frac{183}{360} = \$1{,}715{,}625$

Company pays the bank: $284,375

Illustration 8.2 shows the relation between the dates rates are set and when payments are made for the first two years of the swap.

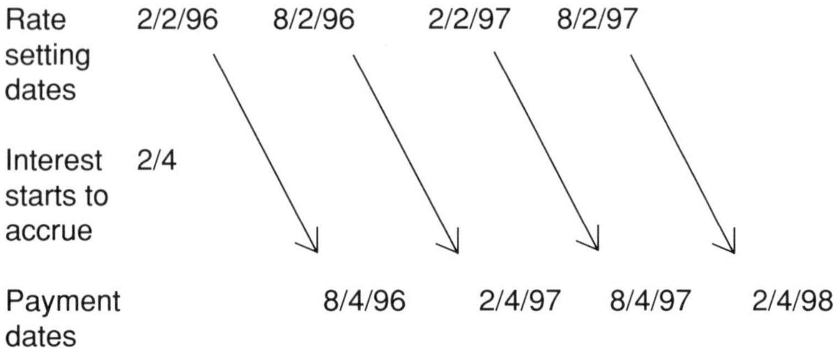

Illustration 8.2 Rate Setting and Payment Dates

Source: Adapted from Burghardt, Belton, Lane, Luce, and McVey, *Eurodollar Futures and Options*, Chicago, Probus Publishing Company, 1991, p. 72.

Business Day Convention: The convention describes what happens when one of the dates falls on a weekend or holiday. Normally, you move to the next business day. The "modified following business day" convention says that you move to the next business day unless that goes into the next month, in which case you go back to the last business day in the month. Although there are a number of date conventions, "modified following" is the most popular because it corresponds to most loan agreements. You have the choice of which convention to use in your swap.

PRICING

Interest rate swaps are priced two ways: U.S. Treasury note plus a swap spread or a strip of Eurodollar futures contracts. The two methods produce the same results. If they did not, professional dealers would buy the cheaper swap and sell the more expensive swap until the swap rate produced by adding a Treasury rate to a swap spread was equal to the swap rate produced by a strip of Eurodollar contracts. Although transactions costs exist, they are not significant.

FUTURES

In the previous chapter, we saw how it is possible to string together Eurodollar futures contracts to generate a single rate. (See Note 1 to Chapter 7.) In our example, we produced a six-month FRA rate and a one-year rate. The same principles apply if you want to generate a five-year swap rate. A five-year swap is a combination of 20 futures contracts plus a Libor deposit rate at the beginning of the period. Pricing according to Eurodollar futures makes it very apparent that the swap rate effectively discounts future cash flows. The futures prices are discount rates on the zero-coupon curve.

Because you can replicate the principal features of a swap with a strip of Eurodollar futures contracts, you have the choice of hedging your exposures with swaps or with futures. If you use swaps, you can tailor the hedge to fit your exposure precisely. Futures settle on only four dates during the year, and the only rate index that is liquid for longer terms is Libor. Tracking a swap contract is a quarterly exercise; tracking futures must be done daily. Once put in place, a swap contract does not have to be adjusted. The numbers of future contracts need to be adjusted as rates move.

Futures, on the other hand, can be less expensive to use than swaps, and the credit of the futures exchange is stronger than most banks. Most companies use swaps and other over-the-counter derivatives because of the precision of the hedge and because their hedging activities are not large enough to justify the operational overhead associated with futures. They feel, and rightly so, that competition among derivatives dealers, with their economies of scale, has sufficiently narrowed the cost difference between swaps and futures.

TREASURIES

Pricing according to the treasury rate plus the swap spread is easier than calculating a futures strip. It's simple addition. Also it makes it clear that the fixed rate on a swap is the equivalent of a coupon on a fixed rate bond. Similarly, the rate on the floating leg is equivalent to the coupon on a floating rate note. Think of the swap transaction in the following terms: you issue a fixed rate bond, receive the principal amount today, make interim fixed interest payments, and repay the principal at maturity. *Simultaneously,* you invest in a floating rate note, pay out principal today, receive a variable rate of interest over the life of the note, and receive the principal at maturity. The principal payments and receipts cancel out. The interest flows remain. This is the swap.

From one to five years, even when swaps are quoted on the basis of a Treasury rate plus swap spread, they are most often priced and hedged by the dealer on the basis of Eurodollar futures contracts. Beyond five years, where large amounts are involved, the Treasury rate plus spread is the usual way of pricing and hedging.

SPREADS

Influences on the level and movement of swap spreads are not as obvious as those that affect interest rates in general. A number of factors affect swap spreads. One factor is the quality spreads at which companies of different rating can borrow from a bank or a public market. The example of the AAA and BBB companies illustrates into what range the numbers might fall. Both parties found a swap spread of 45 basis points was profitable. However, a spread of 61 basis points would be unattractive to the BBB company, and a spread of 34 basis points would be unattractive to the AAA company. As we saw in Chapter 6, swap spreads vary over time, and the difference between highly rated and poorly rated companies also changes over time.

Rate expectations are another influence on spreads. If people think interest rates are going to rise, companies will be inclined to pay the fixed rate in the swap to lock in their cost of funds. This action will raise the level of the swap spread. Similarly, if people think that interest rates are going to fall, companies will be disinclined to pay the fixed rate in a swap. They will be more inclined to swap fixed rate bonds into floating rate. This action will decrease the level of the swap spread.

The Eurodollar futures market is the most important influence on spreads. It is used for speculation on interest rate movements and hedging corporate and portfolio exposures. Additionally, this market serves as a proxy for financial institution quality spreads. If Eurodollar futures prices move down (rates move up) and treasuries are unchanged, swap spreads will increase.

Companies tend to focus intently on swap spreads when hedging exposures. Often this focus detracts from the attention they should be paying to the absolute level of interest rates. As a result, many companies lock in at the wrong time. While the level of swap spreads is certainly important, it is dwarfed in significance by volatility of the absolute level of rates.

BREAK-EVEN ANALYSIS

When the yield curve has a positive slope, you know before you enter into the swap that you will be paying a higher interest rate. Let's assume the fixed rate for a five-year swap is 8 percent and six-month Libor is 6.8 percent. For the first six months of the swap, therefore, you will be paying an additional 1.25 percent. Before committing to the swap transaction, you should analyze what pattern of interest rates make the transaction worthwhile. You want to know the conditions under which you can make up for the initial costs.

A break-even analysis is a useful tool.[2] The break-even rate is the one to which Libor must rise, and remain at, for a swap to have zero cost. If Libor stays below the break-even rate, you will have been better off not to have done the swap. If Libor rises above the break-even rate, the swap will hold down interest expense. Illustration 8.3 shows the framework for this analysis. Only the first three years of the swap are shown; normally, you would calculate the entire five years. Illustration 8.3 shows that, in the first 18 months of the swap, the break-even rate rises rapidly as floating rates climb. It falls thereafter. By the end of 36 months, the swap will have been beneficial even if rates go down to 7.90 percent, below the fixed rate, and stay there for the final 24 months of the swap.

Months	**0 (%)**	**6 (%)**	**12 (%)**	**18 (%)**	**24 (%)**	**30 (%)**	**36 (%)**
Fixed rate	8.0	8.0	8.0	8.0	8.0	8.0	8.0
Libor f'cast	6.8 (set)	7.5	8.0	8.5	8.8	9.0	9.5
Current period saving		(1.2)	(0.5)	0	0.5	0.8	1.0
Accrued saving			(1.2)	(1.8)	(1.9)	(1.5)	(0.8)
Total saving		(1.2)	(1.7)	(1.8)	(1.4)	(0.7)	0.2
Break-even rate		8.3	8.4	8.5	8.5	8.3	7.9

Illustration 8.3 Break-Even Rate

The *Libor forecast* is your own forecast or your bank's, whichever you wish to use.

Current Period Savings: This category shows the results of the rates set in the previous period. The 6-month column shows the difference between the fixed rate and the first rate set of 6.8 percent. The 12-month column shows the difference between the fixed rate and the forecast rate of 7.5 percent.

Accrued Savings: The total savings from the previous period are carried forward and adjusted by the forecasted Libor rate to account for carrying costs. For example, in the 18-month column:

$$1.8\% = (1.7\% \times 8.0\% \times 6/12) + 1.7\%.$$

Total Savings: The sum of current period and accrued savings.

The break-even analysis gives a clearer picture of the costs and benefits of the swap. With this analysis, you can take any interest rate scenario and test the efficiency of a proposed hedge.

VALUATION OF SWAPS

Three years after you enter into the swap, revenues have exceeded expectations. You are planning to pay back the five-year loan two years early. And you no longer need the swap because the exposure will be gone. Since interest rates have gone up, you believe the swap must have some value. You reason that the swap has two years to go; two-year swap rates are 10 percent, and the company has effectively issued debt at 8 percent—2 percent below the current level. Therefore, the swap must be worth something on the order of 2 percent on $50 million for two years, or roughly $2 million. Using 10 percent as a discount rate, that is about $1,650,000.

The swap dealer will fine tune the calculation by estimating what the future flows of the swap will be. The flows on the fixed side are known. To estimate the flows on the floating side, the dealer derives a series of six-month forward rates from the current yield curve. A comparison of these forward rates and the fixed rates gives the net rate to be paid. With that information, flows can be estimated. Each flow is then discounted to today. The amount the swap dealer would pay you to unwind the swap is $1,176,000, $476,000 below your estimate. There are two reasons for the difference: size and timing of the cash flows and the discount rates used.

You assumed that all of the net cash flows would be the same for the next two years; the swap dealer calculated each one separately along the forward curve. You used the discount rate that applied to the flow at the end of two years for all of the cash flows. The dealer used four different discount rates (the zero-coupon rates), one for each flow. The calculation shows the importance of considering each cash flow individually and relying on the forward curve, rather than the yield curve, when calculating swap values after the trade date. Illustration 8.4 shows the difference between the two methods of estimating the value of a swap in mid-life. The math is in Note 3.

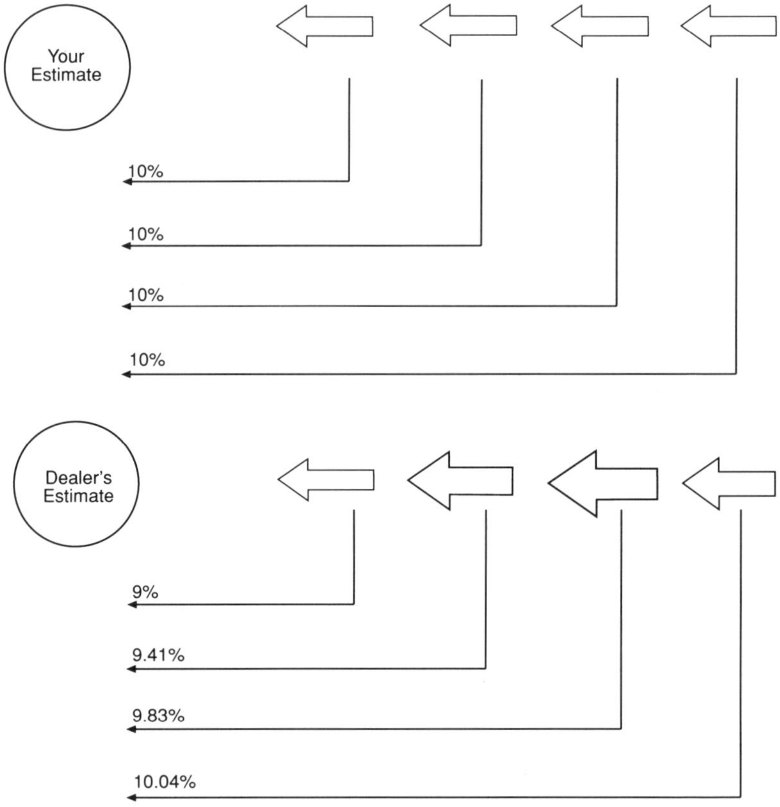

Illustration 8.4 Swap Valuation

NOTES

1. "ISDA Surveys of Swaps Activity, Outstandings, Replacement Costs," *ISDA News*, June/July 1995, p.l.

2. Adapted from an unpublished paper and computer program by John Kerr and Steve Thunem, *Interest Rate Swap Analysis Program*, 1986.

3. The table on the next page gives the results of the calculations for unwinding the swap.

Table 8.2 Payment Frequency and Interest Rates

Period (months)	Yield Curve (%)	Forward Curve/ Floating Rate Estimate (%)	Fixed Swap Coupon (%)	Percent Each Six Months (%)	Future Dollar Cash Flows ($000)	Discount of Dollar Cash fFlows by Zero-Coupon Curve ($000)
6	9.0	9.0	8.0	0.50	250	239
12	9.4	9.4	8.0	0.70	350	320
18	9.8	9.7	8.0	0.85	425	369
24	10.0	9.2	8.0	0.60	300	248
						1,176

CHAPTER 9

How to Execute Cap and Floor Transactions

Caps protect you against a rise in interest rates. Floors protect you against a fall in interest rates. Both allow you to enjoy beneficial interest rates—low rates if you are borrowing, high rates if you are investing. And, you are able to choose the interest rate level at which you want the protection to begin. For this protection, you pay a premium at the start of the transaction. This up-front premium has made caps and floors less popular than swaps. On March 31, 1995, the outstanding volume of caps and floors transacted was about 20 percent of the volume of swaps; nevertheless, caps and floors are well suited and quite useful in a number of exposure situations.

In this chapter, we'll look at how caps and floors offset interest rate exposures. To do that, we'll see how

- caps and floors are priced
- to choose the appropriate level of rate protection
- to deal with premium aversion
- to analyze and choose among swaps, caps, and combinations of the two

Let's assume your company borrows $50 million from its bank to finance expansion. The loan, for five years, amortizes after the first two years, is priced at prime, and interest and principal are payable quarterly. Because your firm operates on rather thin margins, your banker insists on interest rate protection so that a rise in interest rates does not endanger the firm, and, consequently, the repayment of the loan. The yield curve is steep, so you are not inclined to enter into a swap and immediately begin paying higher long term rates. You, therefore, decide to investigate an interest rate cap.

CAP TRANSACTION

The following are details of the cap transaction you are considering:

Notional Amount:	$50 million for two years, thereafter quarterly amortization to zero at the end of year 5
Trade Date:	Feb. 2, 1997
Effective Date:	Feb. 4, 1997
Termination Date:	Feb. 4, 2002
Fixed Rate Payer:	Company
Fixed Rate Payment Dates:	Apr. 4, Jul. 4, Oct. 4, Jan. 4
Floating Rate Payer:	Bank
Cap Rate:	11%
Floating Rate Payment Dates:	Apr. 4, Jul. 4, Oct. 4, Jan. 4
Floating Rate for Initial Calculation Period:	8%
Floating Rate Option:	Prime, Federal Reserve H.15 *Statistical Report*

Floating Rate Day Count Fraction:	Actual/365
Method of Averaging:	Weighted
Business Date Convention:	Modified following business day
Premium Amount:	$425,000

Notional Amount: Because derivatives methodology is able to price individual cash flows, it is possible to exactly match any established principal payment schedule. In this case, the amount of the cap will be $50,000,000 for the first eight quarters; in the 9th quarter, it will be $45,833,333; in the 10th quarter, it will be $41,666,667, and so on. The pricing methodology makes it possible to construct a cap or a swap for the "roller coaster" schedules experienced by retailers heavily dependent on Christmas and Easter sales. (See Illustration 9.1.)

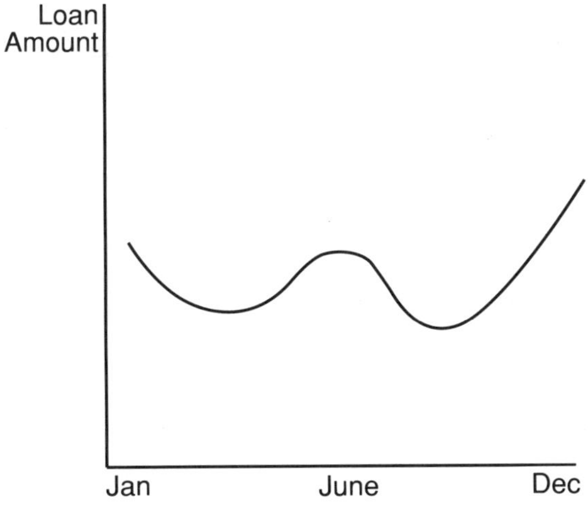

Illustration 9.1 Roller Coaster

Effective Date: As with swaps, the date on which the calculation of the rate average begins is two days after the date of the trade.

Cap Rate: You are considering a level of protection that is above the current level of prime (8 percent), and above the current level of a five-year prime swap (9 percent). The premium for an 8 percent cap is $1,650,000; the premium for a 9 percent cap is $1,100,000. Factors that influence the choice of the cap level are your interest rate expectations and how strongly they are held, the interest rate level at which you begin to have financial difficulties because of the size of your interest expense, and the size of the premium in relation to the protection offered. Later in this chapter, we will look at selecting the appropriate level of protection.

Recall that in Chapter 7 we strung together a series of futures to create a swap. The process of pricing fluctuating amounts is to weight the forward prices by the amount being hedged. It is misleading to attempt to price an amortizing swap or cap, and especially a roller-coaster swap or cap, from standard period rates.

Floating Rate Option: The H.15 *Statistical Report* is published weekly by the Federal Reserve. The daily figures are averaged to arrive at a rate for the period.

Method of Averaging: There are two different averaging conventions: "weighted average," which takes the average of all the days in the month, using Friday's rate for Saturday and Sunday; or "simple average," which takes the average of only the business days in the month. Most companies choose the first convention, because that is the basis on which they pay interest on their loans.

Payment Dates: It is usual to settle two days after the end of the quarter. On the payment date, the bank will make the following calculation:

Cap payout=
Amount of the cap × (average prime rate – cap rate) × 91/360

If the average prime rate is higher than the cap rate, you will receive a payout from the bank. If the average prime rate is lower than the cap rate, there is no payout, nothing happens. If the average prime rate for the quarter were 11.75 percent, your interest cost for the quarter would be:

Cost of bank loan:	11.75%
Cap payout:	(0.75%)
Net rate:	11.00% (excluding premium)

If the average prime rate for the following quarter were 10 percent, your interest cost for the quarter would be:

Cost of bank loan:	10.00%
Cap payout:	0
Net rate:	10.00% (excluding premium)

Premium: Payable two days after the trade date, the premium is usually expressed as a percentage of the amount of the cap or floor. For example, if the premium on a $65 million, four-year cap is 1.10 percent, the amount of the premium is $715,000. It is not possible to apply the same math to a cap where the amount covered fluctuates throughout the life of the cap. As we will see in the next section on pricing, a different premium will apply to each period and each amount.

PRICING

Caps and floors are a series of options strung together to cover a period of time. We'll first look at basic option pricing, and then see how this relates to caps and floors. An option is an instrument that grants the buyer a right without any obligations. The most common options give the buyer of the option the right to buy a specific stock, at a specified price, during a specified period, upon payment of a premium. For example, the right to buy 100 shares of IBM, at $95, until December 16, for a premium of $5. In another example, the buyer of the option has the right to sell a $100,000 30-year treasury bond, at 99, on June 18, for a premium of $2500.

BASIC OPTION PRICING

Three elements affect the price of an option, they are the

- relation of the option price (called strike price) to the price at which the instrument is currently trading
- amount of time between the purchase of the option and when it can be exercised
- volatility of the price

If the option price is the same as the price at which the instrument is trading, the option is "at-the-money." If you buy an option to buy a stock and the strike price is higher than the current price, the option is "out-of-the-money." If the strike price is lower than the current price, the option is "in-the-money." These terms describe the intrinsic value of the option.

For example, if coffee is selling for $7 a pound, an option to buy it for $5 a pound sometime in the next six months is worth at least $2. The option to buy it for $7 is currently worth nothing. The option to buy it for $9 is currently $2 out-of-the-money. The premiums track the intrinsic value. When you consider the option to *sell*, however, the logic of what is out-of-the-money and in-the-money reverses itself, as do the premium levels. The option to sell coffee at $9 has an intrinsic value of $2, whereas the option to buy at that price is out-of-the-money.

The more time the price or rate on a financial instrument has to move up and down, the more companies are willing to pay for options on that instrument because it is more likely that the instrument will move through the strike price and make the option valuable.

The more the price or rate on a financial instrument moves up and down, the more companies are willing to pay for options on that instrument, because it becomes more likely that the instrument will move through the strike price and make the option valuable. When interest rates are volatile, options are more expensive. Unlike intrinsic value and time, volatility is not directly observable. It has to be calculated. Different banks use different formulas for calculating it. Therefore, when buying a derivative that incorporates an option, you should shop a number of dealers before buying.

Illustration 9.2 shows the premium pricing diagram for options. Each element of the premium is shown in relation to the price of the underlying instrument, though they are not shown in proper proportion. Note that volatility is at its peak when the option is at-the-money. Intrinsic value begins to become the most important consideration when the underlying instrument moves in-the-money.

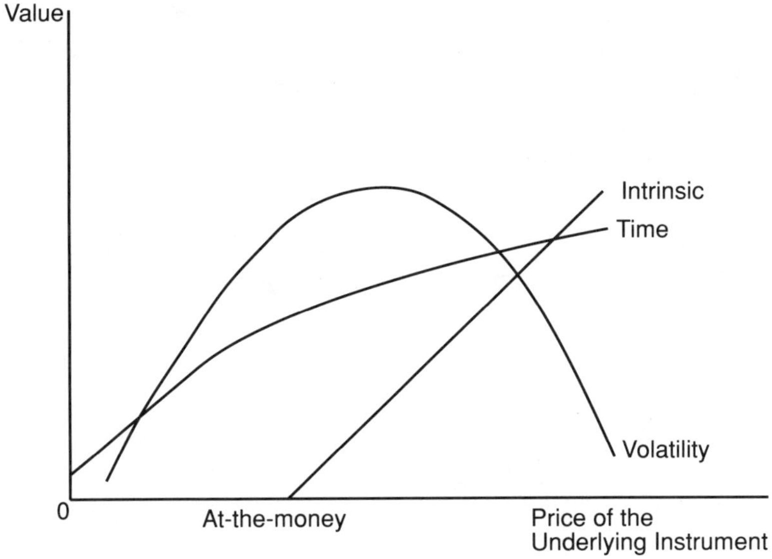

Illustration 9.2 Premium Pricing

Buying a floor is equivalent to buying the right to earn a specified rate on an investment. If the market rate goes below the specified rate, you still earn that rate. But when you think about caps, think about buying the right to sell a loan at a specified rate. In a world where prime is 12 percent, the right to sell a loan at 11 percent is worth 1 percent. A borrower clearly would pay somewhere close to that for an 11 percent loan.

APPLICATION OF OPTION PRICING TO CAPS AND FLOORS

Caps and floors are composed of strings of options called *caplets* and *floorlets*. In our example, the cap consists of a caplet on a three-month loan starting today, another caplet on a three-month loan starting three months from today, another caplet on a three-month loan starting six months from today, and so on. Each of those three-month loans has its own forward rate. Therefore, when thinking about the intrinsic value of a cap and how pricing is affected, the cap rate must be compared to the forward rates, not to the current level of prime.

Illustration 9.3 shows a curve of forward rates, a cap, and a floor. Notice that the cap starts out being priced out-of-the-money, but is priced in-the-money in the later years. Conversely, the floor starts out being priced in-the-money, but is increasingly priced out-of-the-money in the later years.

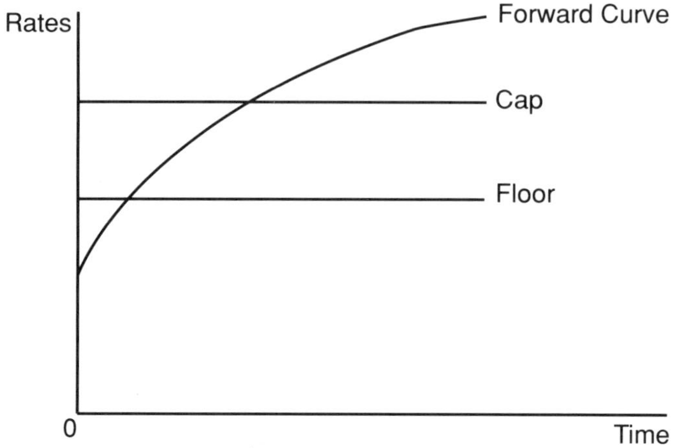

Illustration 9.3 Pricing Caps and Floors—1

Illustration 9.4 shows a negatively sloped forward curve with a cap and floor. The pricing is the opposite of the previous illustration. In this case, the floor moves from being priced out-of-the-money to being priced in-the-money, and the cap moves from being priced in-the-money to being priced out-of-the-money. It follows that when the forward curve is positive and steep, caps will be expensive. Caps will be inexpensive when the forward curve is negatively sloped. It is the other way around for floors.

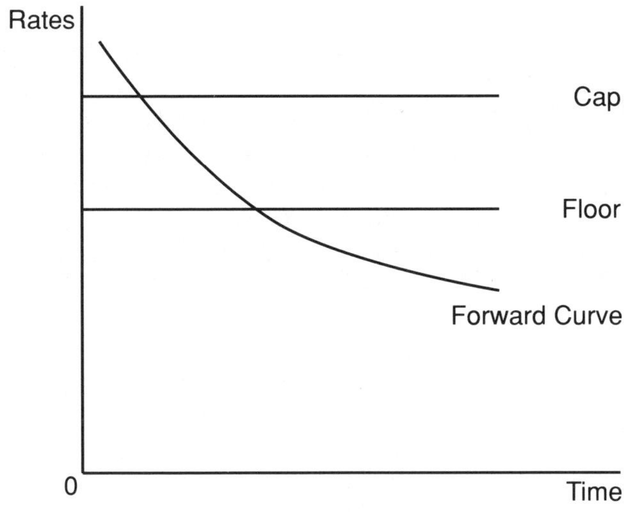

Illustration 9.4 Pricing of Caps and Floors—2

CHOOSING A STRIKE RATE FOR A CAP OR FLOOR

You choose a cap or floor strike rate depending on the amount of the premium, where you believe interest rates are going, how firmly you hold this belief, and the level of interest rates that will cause financial distress to the company. First, you need to determine the annual cost of the cap or floor. The premium is spread out over the life of the cap agreement, adjusted for the frequency of the settlement periods and for being paid entirely at the start of the transaction. The formula for amortizing the premium is in Note 2.

Table 9.1 attempts to capture the considerations that go into choosing a cap level. You are looking at the first two years of a five-year cap on prime, with quarterly settlements. The table compares two different cap levels and an unhedged position. The prime rate is your forecast for the period. The basis for the comparison is the sum of the present values of the interest rates that you pay over the period. The best alternative is that with the lowest value. In this example, it is the unhedged alternative. Among the two cap levels, the 11 percent cap is the best value. This methodology allows you to consider one or many interest rate forecasts. The firmness with which you hold an interest rate view will dictate how many scenarios you run. Those with the least firmly held view should examine a number of alternative forecasts.

Referring to the chart, the all-in cap rate is the strike rate plus the amortized premium. The all-in floating rate is the forecast of prime plus the amortized premium. The rate paid will be the lower of the floating rate or the cap rate. The present value is the rate paid, discounted by zero curve for Treasuries.

Table 9.1 Comparison of Cap Strike Rates (Figures in %)

Quarter	1	2	3	4	5	6	7	8
Cap Strike	**9.0**							
Premium	**3.4**							
All-in cap rate	10.9	10.9	10.9	10.9	10.9	10.9	10.9	10.9
All-in floating rate (f'cast)	9.9	10.9	11.9	12.9	13.9	12.9	11.9	10.9
Rate paid	9.9	10.9	10.9	10.9	10.9	10.9	10.9	10.9
Present value	9.7	10.5	10.3	10.1	9.9	9.6	9.4	9.2
Sum of PV	78.8							
Cap Strike	**11.0**							
Premium	**1.35**							
All-in cap rate	11.7	11.7	11.7	11.7	11.7	11.7	11.7	11.7
All-in floating rate (f'cast)	8.7	9.7	10.7	11.7	12.7	11.7	10.7	9.7
Rate paid	8.7	9.7	10.7	11.7	11.7	11.7	10.7	9.7
Present value	8.6	9.4	10.9	10.8	10.6	10.4	9.2	8.2
Sum of PV	77.2							
Floating Unhedged								
Floating rate (f'cast)	8.0	9.0	10.0	11.0	12.0	11.0	10.0	9.0
Present value	7.9	8.7	9.5	10.2	10.9	9.7	8.6	7.6
Sum of PV	73.0							

WAYS TO DEAL WITH PREMIUM AVERSION

Most people do not like to pay out premiums up front. There are, however, a number of alternatives: (1) a collar, (2) a corridor, and (3) a digital cap. As you will see, the alternatives for reducing the premium will entail accepting other risks.

COLLAR

Collar is the term for the combination of a cap and a floor. You buy a cap to protect yourself against rising rates, and benefit if rates are lower than the cap level. But if you are willing to give up some of that benefit, you can earn a premium by selling a floor to the bank. When you *buy* a floor, you are compensated when rates go below the floor level. When you *sell* a floor, you make the compensation. Buying a cap and selling a floor effectively put a collar around the interest rates you will pay for a loan. This is depicted in Illustration 9.5, where the cost of funds would range between 6.50 percent and 9 percent regardless of the course of future rate.

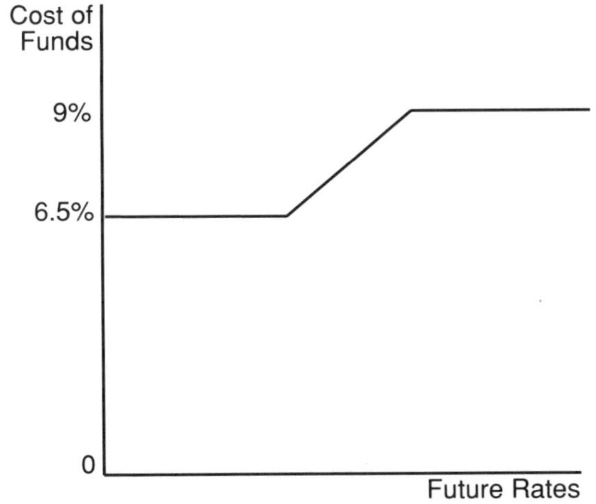

Illustration 9.5 Collar

The premium received for selling the floor may or may not offset the cap premium. It is possible to construct a collar where the premium paid on the cap and the premium received on the floor offset one another. The result is a *zero-cost collar*, and you pay nothing for rate protection. The ability to construct an attractive zero-cost collar is easier if the forward curve is not steeply sloped.

In the section on pricing, we looked at the relation of cap and floor premiums to the forward curve. Illustration 9.6 shows that when the forward curve is steep, the interest rate range of the collar is very tight. When the forward curve is relatively flat, the interest rate range of the collar is much wider.

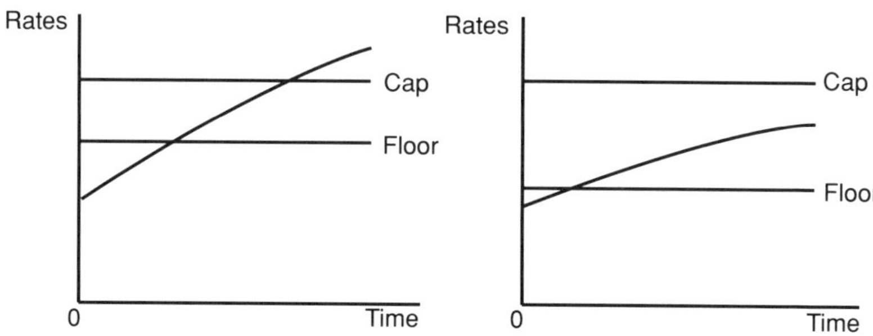

Illustration 9.6 Collar Width in Two Forward Curve Scenarios

A *participating rate agreement* is a variation on this theme. It partially offsets the premium on a $50 million cap by selling a floor on $25 million. It allows you to participate more from lower interest rates. Compare Illustration 9.7 with the collar in Illustration 9.5.

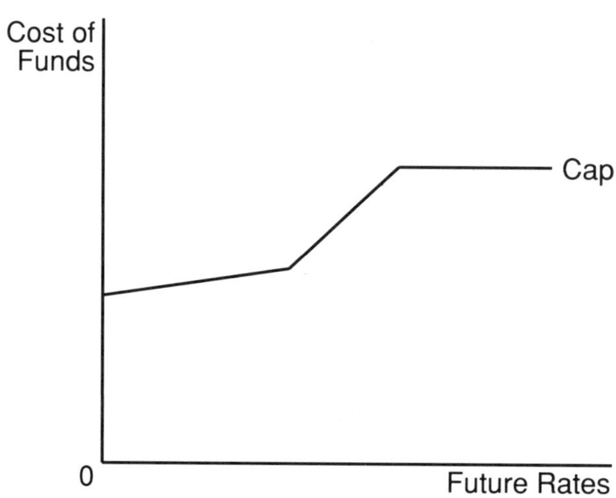

Illustration 9.7 Participating Rate Agreement

The benefit of a collar and its variants is that the premium on a cap is offset. The risk is that your company will pay more for its funds when rates are low. This is an appropriate risk if your company is able to perform well in an economy characterized by low interest rates, and if it is not in a competitive industry characterized by large amounts of debt.

CORRIDOR

A *corridor* consists of buying a cap at one strike rate and selling another cap at a higher strike rate. The reason is to partially offset the premium paid on the purchased cap with the premium earned on the cap sold. Illustration 9.8 shows that the cost of funds flattens out at the rate at which you buy a cap, 9 percent, but then starts to rise again at the rate where you sell a cap, 12 percent.

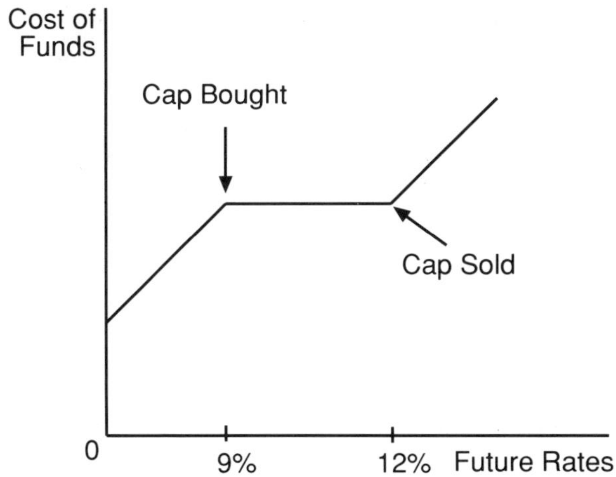

Illustration 9.8 Corridor

To enter into a transaction of this nature, you must have a very firm view on interest rates, because you are giving up rate protection at the very time rates are heading higher. Or, you are in one of the few businesses that can pass costs on to its customers.

DIGITAL CAP

A *digital cap* has a predefined payoff if interest rates go above the cap level. For example, let's assume the cap strike rate is 9 percent and the predefined payoff is 1 percent of the capped amount. If interest rates go to 11 percent, the cap buyer receives 1 percent; if interest rates go to 9.2 percent, the cap buyer receives 1 percent. The advantage of the digital cap is that the premium is less expensive than a standard cap. However, the protection is less and you are not protected against high rate levels. Before entering into a digital cap transaction, you need to have a definite view about the range of future interest rates, and tailor the predefined payout accordingly.

A way to reduce the premium for a standard cap is to sell a digital cap. It is worth considering because it operates on the same principle as a corridor, but is a more conservative approach for a borrower. To see how it reduces premium and still provides protection, assume you buy a 9 percent standard cap and then sell a digital cap at the same level with a 1 percent payout. The net premium is 0.45 percent. Table 9.2 shows how the combination works under different rate conditions.

Table 9.2 Buy a Standard Cap, Sell a Digital Cap

Market Rates (%)	Premium (%)	Standard Cap (%)	Digital Cap (%)	Net Rate (%)
7.00	0.45	0	0	7.45
9.20	0.45	(0.20)	1.00	10.45
11.00	0.45	(2.00)	1.00	10.45

Illustration 9.9 shows that at the level of 9.45 percent, interest expense increases immediately by 1 percent, but goes no higher. Compare this to Illustration 9.8 where, above 12 percent, you pay the higher market rates.

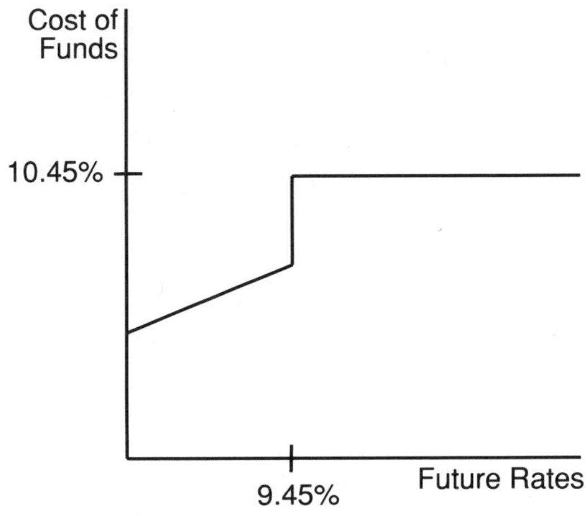

Illustration 9.9 Buy a Standard Cap and Sell a Digital Cap

COMBINATIONS AND PERMUTATIONS OF CAPS AND SWAPS

It is possible to engineer derivatives to produce a multitude of hedging alternatives for companies. The key to choosing an alternative is to match the cash flows of the hedge to those of the exposure, and to test when rates change, the hedge compensates you for any changes in the cash flows. Some of the standard combinations and permutations of caps and swaps offered in the market are: partial swaps, out-of-the-money swaps, and step-up and step-down swaps and caps.

PARTIAL SWAPS

Partial swaps cover a percentage of the exposure. The other portion of the exposure is not hedged. You chose the percentage to cover. The advantage is that you are able to enjoy some of the benefit of lower rates—at the risk of paying more if rates go up.

You also can use a partial swap to hedge the exposure of tax-free floating rate debt. The rate on the debt is a fraction of the rate on fully taxable debt; the fraction depends on federal and state tax rates. The amount of the swap is reduced by that fraction. This hedge protects you against adverse movements in interest rates. It does not, however, protect you against changes in tax rates. The way to protect against changes in tax rates and interest rates is to enter into a swap where the floating rate index is tied to tax free rates. Two indices are commonly used—JJKenny and PSA. The PSA index is more popular because it is the average of a couple of hundred outstanding tax-free floating rate notes, whereas JJ Kenny is the result of a survey of dealers.

OUT-OF-THE-MONEY SWAP

The rate for an out-of-the-money swap is higher than the current market rate. A 10 percent swap rate is 1.50 percent out-of-the-money if the current market rate is 8.50 percent. When you enter into this transaction, you will be paid a lump sum equal to the present value of 1.50 percent times the notional amount of the swap. With the lump sum, you might buy a cap and have no out-of-pocket cost. This produces yet another profile of interest rate risk protection. The combination of a swap and a cap is called a *participating hedge*. It has the certainty of a swap at higher rates with some of the ability to take advantage of lower rates that is characteristic of caps. The downside to the participating swap is that the initial swap rate is higher than what it would be otherwise.

Illustration 9.10 compares a swap, cap, partial swap, and participating hedge. It is a good illustration of the tradeoffs you need to consider when choosing a hedging instrument—certainty, what rate levels will prevail, cost of the hedge, and affordability. Depending on your view of future rates, you could make a case for each alternative.

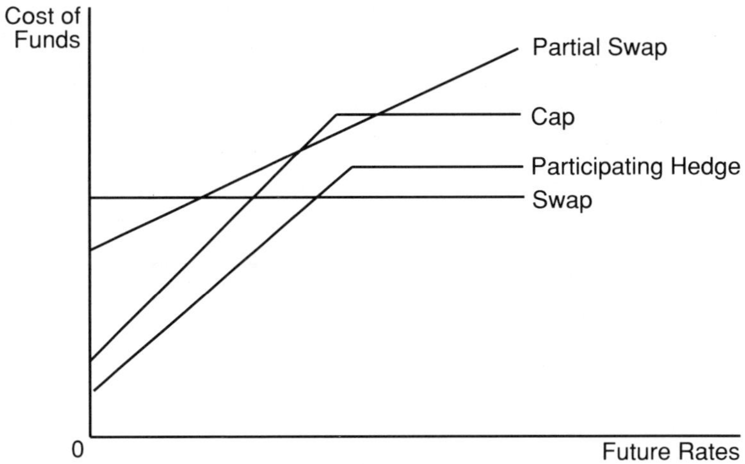

Illustration 9.10 Swaps, Caps, and Combinations

STEP-UP AND STEP-DOWN SWAPS AND CAPS

Step-up and *step-down* swaps and caps are derivatives whose rates change over the life of the transaction, but in a way that is designed from the start. The derivative is fashioned to address the cash flow characteristics of a company or a project. If your company's cash flow is tight in the first years of a project, a step-up swap is appropriate.

Table 9.3 shows the interest rate levels you can afford, current market swap rates, and the step-up solution. The underlying approach is to start from your exposure situation and tailor a solution around it. The bank prices the step-up swap so that on a present value basis it has the same value as a standard five-year swap.

Table 9.3 Step-up Swap

Year	Affordable Rate (%)	Market Swap Rate (%)	Step-up Solution (%)
1	7	8.50	7.00
2	8	9.00	8.00
3	9	9.25	9.00
4	11	9.50	10.50
5	14	10.00	13.00

NOTES

1. *Swaps Monitor*, Vol. 9, No. 5, January 1, 1996, p. 6.

2. The formula for converting an up front premium to an effective annual percentage cost is given by:

$$\left(1 + \frac{P}{\dfrac{1 - \dfrac{1}{(1+r/s)^{n \times s}}}{r/s}} \right)^{s} - 1$$

where:
P = premium
r = discount rate
n = number of years of the cap or floor
s = number of settlement periods per year

As an example, let's look at a seven percent three-year floor on three-month Libor, settlement quarterly, with a premium of 4.20 percent, and assume a discount rate of 6 percent. The effective annual percentage cost of the floor is 1.55 percent.

$$\left(1 + \frac{.0420}{\dfrac{1 - \dfrac{1}{1+(.06/4)^{3 \times 4}}}{.06/4}} \right)^{4} - 1$$

This is not a simple formula, but you can see if your result is reasonable by comparing it to the result of dividing the premium by the number of years. The formula will give a somewhat higher number. The source for this formula is Kenneth R. Kapner and John F. Marshall, *The Swaps Handbook,* New York, New York Institute of Finance, 1990, pp. 247-249.

CHAPTER 10

How to Read Derivative Rates

When you know how to read derivative rates, you will understand the numbers you are being quoted by derivatives dealers. You can verify the rates you are getting by checking wire services and by tracking the value of your transactions.

When you call a derivatives dealer, you usually get a quote for the transaction you want to do. In this chapter, you will learn to understand a quote that has both bid/offer or buy/sell prices or rates. The size of the spread between the bid rate and the offer rate is an indication of the liquidity of the market. Tighter spreads exist in more liquid markets. This is important because it gives you a good indication of how easily you can get out of the transaction if you want to. The spread is also an indication of the quality of the dealer. Good dealers quote tight spreads relative to the market.

Three basic rules apply when you are quoted a two-way price, for example, 15-20:

1. If you are selling something or earning interest, you will receive the low price or rate, 15.

2. If you are buying something or paying interest, you will pay the high price or rate, 20.

3. When you add the prices or rates in two markets together to get a combined rate, the resulting spread between the bid-offer or buy-sell will be the sum of the spreads in the two markets. If one market quotes 15-20 and another quotes 10-12, the combined quote is 25-32, a spread of 7.

These basic rules apply to all markets. In this chapter, we look at Treasuries, swaps against Libor, swaps against prime, swaps against commercial paper, FRAs, caps, and floors.

TREASURIES

We'll start with treasuries and then look at rates in the derivatives market. Table 10.1 shows the prices and yields for U.S. Treasury notes from two to 10 years.

Table 10.1 U.S. Treasury Note Prices and Yields

Maturity (Years)	Prices	Yield to Maturity (%)
2	99.28-99.29	5.91-5.93
3	100.04-100.05	6.04-6.06
4		6.13-6.15
5	99.16-99.17	6.22-6.24
7		6.33-6.35
10	99.27-99.28	6.50-6.52

Bond and note prices are written as a whole number, for example, 99, and a number of thirty seconds, for example, 29. This is an industry convention. So a price of 99.29 could be written 99 29/32. The yield to maturity follows the standard decimal convention; 5.91 is equivalent to 5 91/100.

The Treasury issues 2-, 3-, 5-, 10- and 30-year notes. The yield on the 4-year note is interpolated based on the number of days remaining in the most recently issued 3- and 5-year notes. The most recently issued notes are referred to as "on the run." The 7-year note yield is interpolated using the 5- and 10-year notes as reference points.

If you were selling a three-year Treasury note, it would sell at 100.04, a yield to maturity of 6.04 percent. This is rule 1. If you were buying a two-year Treasury note as an investment, you would pay 99.29. The yield to maturity of the note is 5.91 percent. This is rule 2.

SWAPS AGAINST LIBOR

Interest rate swap spreads are quoted as a number of basis points (b.p.), for example, 16 means 0.0016, and they are added to the treasury yield. Unless otherwise stated, swap spread quotes assume that the floating leg of the swap is six-month Libor. Table 10.2 shows swap spreads, Treasury yields, and the resulting swap coupons.

Table 10.2 Swap Coupons

Year	Swap Spreads (b.p.)	Treasury Yields (%)	Swap Coupons (%)
2	16-20	5.91-5.93	6.07-6.13
3	20-24	6.04-6.06	6.24-6.30
4	25-29	6.13-6.15	6.38-6.44
5	28-32	6.22-6.24	6.50-6.56
7	32-35	6.33-6.35	6.65-6.70
10	37-40	6.50-6.52	6.87-6.92

Note that the spread of the swap coupon is the sum of the swap spread and the Treasury spread, as explained in rule 3.

If you want to cover a floating rate exposure for 10 years, you will pay a swap coupon of 6.92 percent, rule 2. If you issued a five-year fixed rate bond and want to swap it back to a floating rate, you will earn 6.50 percent on the five-year swap, which is rule 1.

PRIME SWAPS

Prime is quoted against three-month Libor; it is not quoted directly against a fixed rate. A quote of prime against Libor is called a basis swap. In a basis swap, the parties pay a floating rate of interest, and each is tied to a different index. Table 10.3 shows typical quotes for prime/Libor swaps:

Table 10.3 Prime/Libor Swaps

Maturity (Years)	Prime/Libor (b.p.)	
2	–285	–275
3	–274	–264
4	–267	–257
5	–262	–252
7	–257	–247
10	–250	–240

In the two-year quote, the number on the left means a company receives prime minus 285 basis points and pays Libor. The number on the right means a company pays prime minus 275 basis points and receives Libor. Illustration 10.1 shows how the Libor-based swap coupon is combined with the swap of prime against Libor to produce a swap of prime against a fixed rate. The rates for a two-year swap are used.

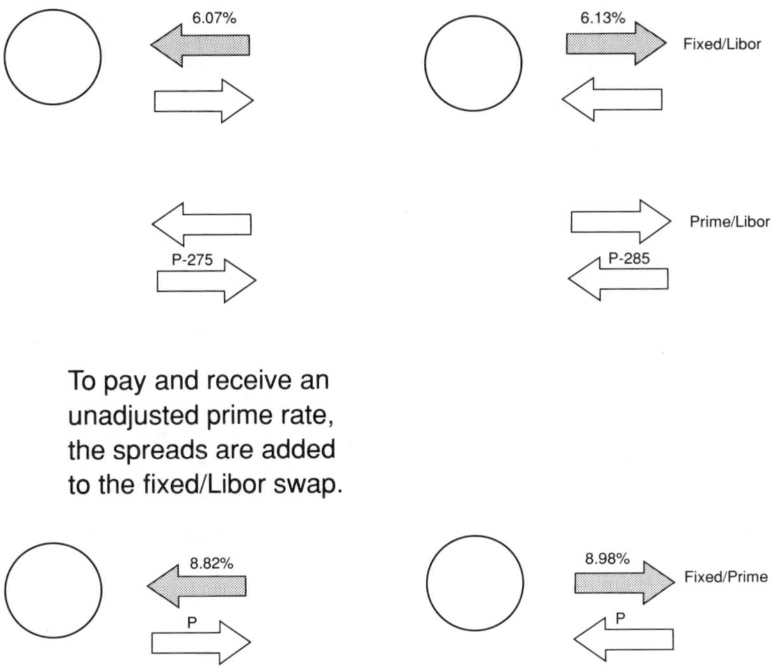

Illustration 10.1 Prime Swap

The easy way to remember this is: since prime is always higher than Libor, the fixed rate against prime must be higher than the fixed rate against Libor; therefore, the prime/Libor swap numbers must be added to the fixed/Libor swap coupon. Rule 3 says the resulting spread must increase, so switch the numbers as quoted and add.

COMMERCIAL PAPER SWAPS

Commercial paper is also quoted against three-month Libor; it is not quoted directly against a fixed rate. Table 10.4 shows typical quotes for commercial paper/Libor swaps.

Table 10.4 Commercial Paper/Libor

Tenor (years)	Commercial Paper/Libor (b.p.)	
2	–1.00	+3.00
3	–0.50	+3.50
4	+0.50	+4.50
5	+1.00	+5.00
7	+2.00	+6.00
10	+3.00	+7.00

In the two-year quote, the number on the left means that you receive the commercial paper rate minus one basis point and pay Libor. The number on the right means that you pay the commercial paper rate plus three basis points and receive Libor.

Illustration 10.2 shows how the commercial paper/Libor swap is combined with a fixed/Libor swap to produce a fixed/commercial paper swap.

To pay or receive an unadjusted commercial paper rate, the numbers are subtracted from the fixed rate. In the case where you are paying the fixed rate on the swap, since it is CP -1, it becomes fixed rate +1.

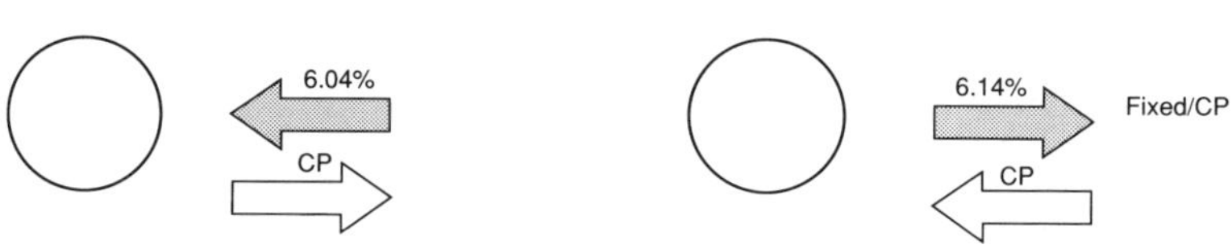

Illustration 10.2 Commercial Paper Swap

The easy way to remember this is: since commercial paper rates are generally lower than Libor, the fixed rate against commercial paper must be lower than the fixed rate against Libor; therefore, the commercial paper/Libor swap numbers must be subtracted from the fixed/Libor swap coupon. Rule 3 says the resulting spread must increase, so switch the numbers as quoted and subtract.

In addition to prime and commercial paper, there are treasury bill/Libor, Fed Funds/Libor, PSA/Libor, and JJKenny/Libor swaps. To find a fixed rate against any of the indices, start with the fixed/Libor swap coupon as a basis and adjust. Knowing where the relative rate levels are, and knowing that the combined spreads must increase, will guide your construction of a quote.

FRAs

In Chapter 7, we talked about buying and selling FRAs to hedge rate exposure, but did not show how FRAs are quoted. A typical run of FRA rates is shown in Table 10.5, though an FRA can be quoted for any period.

Table 10.5 FRA Quotes

Period (months)	FRA Rates (%)
1×4	5.81 – 5.85
2×5	5.78 – 5.82
3×6	5.76 – 5.80
6×9	5.71 – 5.75
1×7	5.83 – 5.87
2×8	5.80 – 5.84
3×9	5.79 – 5.83
6×12	5.83 – 5.87

The period convention is to quote the number of months from today as the first number and the final maturity as the second number.

A 1×4 quote is an FRA starting in 1 month on 3-month money.
A 2×5 quote is an FRA starting in 2 months on 3-month money.
A 6×12 quote is an FRA starting in 6 months on 6-month money.

Using the first quote as an example, if you were an investor protecting your portfolio against a fall in rates in the future, you would sell an FRA at 5.81 percent, as in rule 1. On the other hand, if you were hedging against future borrowing you would buy an FRA at 5.85 percent, as in rule 2.

CAPS AND FLOORS

Cap and floor quotes are fairly straightforward. The vital information is the term, the strike rate, bid, offer, and the rate index. Table 10.6 depicts the extract of a quote sheet for caps and floors.

Table 10.6 Cap and Floor Premiums for Three-Month Libor

Maturity (years)	Cap/Floor	Strike Rate (%)	Bid (%)	Offer (%)
2	Cap	6	0.86	0.90
2	Cap	7	0.34	0.37
2	Cap	8	0.16	0.18
2	Floor	5	0.25	0.28
2	Floor	6	0.95	0.98
2	Floor	7	1.64	1.68

In the first row, if you buy a 6 percent cap to hedge a $50 million two-year loan, you will pay the offer rate of 0.90, rule 2. The premium paid is:

$$\$450{,}000 = 50{,}000{,}000 \times 0.0090$$

A company that sells a cap at 8 percent for two years as part of a corridor will earn a premium of 16 basis points, or $80,000, rule 1.

SOURCES

The sources for rates, except for the caps and floors, are Telerate pages 19901, 19903, and 19906 for August 3, 1995. The information is provided by Market Data Corporation. The data source is Tullett & Tokyo. The cap and floor rates were calculated by the author in August 1995.

CHAPTER 11

Exposure That Starts in the Future

In this chapter, we look at derivatives designed for exposures that start in the future, and subsequently have found a place in managing existing exposures. They are forward swaps, forward caps, and options on swaps called *swaptions*. Most often they are used when companies are issuing new debt or managing existing debt. We'll look at three different exposure situations: (1) you are planning to issue new debt in the public market six months from today, (2) you are looking at ways of managing callable debt you will issue or have issued, and (3) you are attempting to reduce the cost and increase the flexibility of managing existing debt.

ISSUING A FIVE-YEAR NOTE IN THE FUTURE

Your company plans to issue a $200 million, five-year note in six months. You are not certain where rates will be in the next six months, but sense an upward trend and want protection against any significant increases in interest rates. You are thinking about two alternatives: forward swaps that lock in a rate, and swaptions that put a ceiling on a rate but allow you to take advantage of lower rates. First, you assume the hedge and the exposure are perfectly matched; then, since that does not always happen, you look at what can be done when they are not.

FORWARD SWAP

Your first alternative is to enter into a five-year swap to pay a fixed rate six months from today, but with rate and terms set today:

Notional Amount:	$200,000,000
Effective Date:	September 14, 1997
Termination Date:	September 14, 2002
Fixed Rate Payer:	Company
Fixed Rate:	7.50%
Fixed Rate Payer Payment Dates:	March 14, September 14
Fixed Rate Day Count Fraction:	30/360
Floating Rate Payer:	Bank
Floating Rate Payer Payment Dates:	March 14, September 14
First Floating Rate:	N/A
Floating Rate Option:	Six-month Libor, Telerate page 3750
Floating Rate Day Count Fraction:	Actual/360
Business Day Convention:	Modified following business day

The differences between this forward swap and the swaps discussed in Chapter 8 are that the forward swap starts later; the first floating rate is set six months from today, two days prior to the effective date; and the pricing of the fixed rate is different.

SWAPTION

Your second alternative is to buy a six-month option for the right to pay a fixed rate on a five-year swap—a swaption. The rate and terms on the swap are the same as the forward swap. Shown below are the details that describe the option.

Trade Date:	March 12, 1997
Seller:	Bank
Buyer:	Company
Premium:	$2,500,000
Premium Payment Date:	March 14, 1997
Physical Settlement:	Not Applicable
Cash Settlement:	Applicable
Cash Settlement Payment Date:	September 14, 1997
Cash Settlement Amount:	On September 12, 1997, three mutually agreed upon reference dealers will be asked to quote, for value September 14, a buyout value for the swap on which this option is based. The highest amount will be the cash settlement amount.
Option Style:	European
Exercise Period:	September 12, 1997, by 11:00 a.m. notice of exercise must be delivered in writing.

The swaption is an option to enter into the forward swap. For this choice, a premium is paid two days after agreeing to the trade. In this case, a European option was chosen. A *European swaption* can be exercised only on the last day of the option period. If the swap has value at the end of the six-month option period, the company can either enter into the swap or receive the value as a cash settlement. In this example, we have opted for cash settlement, since the swaption is being used to hedge a note issue. There is no intention of entering into the swap.

ANALYSIS AND COMPARISON

The forward swap hedges the exposure because the value of the five-year swap will go up if interest rates go up. At the time the note is issued, you reverse the swap and realize the gain in cash.

The gain compensates you for the increased cost of the note. If interest rates have gone down, the value of the five-year swap will have gone down and the note will be issued at a lower rate. But that will be offset by the cost of reversing the swap. By entering into a forward swap, you have effectively fixed the rate of the note issuance today. Even though the period is longer, the dynamics of a forward swap and an FRA are exactly the same.

When you enter into the transaction, you also can arrange a buyout formula with the bank. The formula specifies how the Treasury rate and the swap spread will be determined, and what rate sources will be used. This protects you from arbitrary pricing when you reverse the swap.

The swaption also hedges the exposure because its value will go up if interest rates go up. When the note is issued, the swaption will be sold. The gain from selling the swaption compensates you for the increased cost of the note issued. The difference between the forward swap and swaption is that if interest rates go down, you let the swaption expire and issue notes at lower rates. Buying a swaption protects you from rising rates, but allows you to take advantage of lower rates. It works just like the caps on short term money we discussed in Chapter 9.

The following example shows a forward swap and a swaption. The five-year swap rate is 7 percent, and that is also the rate at which you would be able to issue a note today. The forward swap rate is 7.50 percent. You are thinking about a swaption where the strike rate is at-the-money, equal to the forward swap rate. (In the same way that you analyzed the choice of cap strike rates in Chapter 9, you can analyze different swaption strike rates.) The swaption premium is 1.22 percent; amortized over five years, that is 0.30 percent per year.

At the end of six months, two possibilities for the five-year swap rate and the note issuing rate are:

If at 8 percent:

	Forward Swap (%)	Swaption (%)
Note rate:	8.00	8.00
Gain from derivative:	(0.50)	(0.50)
Swaption premium:		0.30
Cost of funds:	7.50	7.80

If at 6 percent:

	Forward Swap (%)	Swaption (%)
Note rate:	6.00	6.00
Loss from derivative:	1.50	0
Swaption premium:		0.30
Cost of funds:	7.50	6.30

It is clear that you cannot fix the issuing rate at the current level, only at the forward swap rate. If you were very sure that rates were going to rise, it might be tempting to double the amount of the forward swap from $200 million to $400 million. This way you would gain 0.50 percent on $400 million, or 1 percent on $200 million, and the issuing cost in six months would be the same as today. If, for some reason, you were wrong and rates went down to 6 percent, your company would end up with a loss of 1.50 percent on $400 million, or 3 percent on $200 million, and its issuing rate would be 9 percent. This would result in additional interest expense of $15 million over five years.

MATCHING NOTE ISSUANCE AND THE HEDGE

What happens if the rate at which you can issue notes does not move in the same way as swap rates? What if the five-year note is issued before the forward swap is due to start?

If swap rates and note rates do not move together, you could be underhedged. For example, note rates change 1 percent, swap rates only change 0.80 percent. Swap coupons move with treasury rates and swap spreads. Your note rates move with treasury rates and quality spreads. Only a weak connection, however, exists between the movement of swap spreads and the movement of quality spreads. (Illustrations 11.1 and 11.2 show their movement over the last four years.) The most that can be said is that the two spreads generally follow the same trend in the medium term, although sometimes they move in opposite directions. The bottom line is that forward swaps and swaptions effectively hedge the movement of the underlying treasury, and are weak hedges against movement in quality spreads.

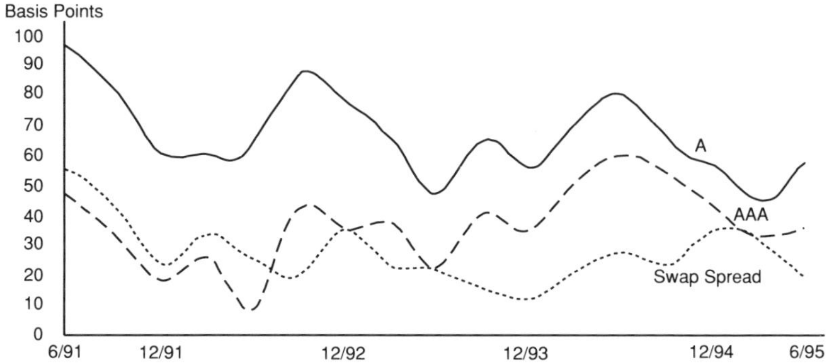

Illustration 11.1 Swap Spreads and Quality Spreads—Two Years

Sources: Data from Bloomberg, *U.S. Fair Value Sector*, IN02, H15T2, August 2, 1995, and V.K. Ranganathan, *Interest Rate Trends and Comparisons*, data base, September 1995.

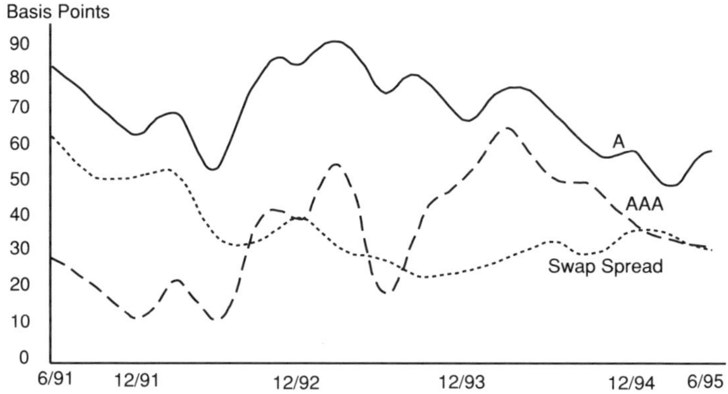

Illustration 11.2 Swap Spreads and Quality Spreads—Five Years

Sources: Data from Bloomberg, *U.S. Fair Value Sector*, IN05, H15T5, August 2, 1995, and V.K. Ranganathan, *Interest Rate Trends and Comparisons*, data base, September 1995.

If a company finds that swap spreads and their quality spreads frequently move in different directions, the alternative is to hedge only the movement in the underlying Treasury note. You may accomplish this with *Treasury locks*, the equivalent of the forward swap, and *options on Treasuries*, the equivalent of the swaption.

Both the forward swap and the swaption are set for September 14. What happens if a window of opportunity opens for note issuance on August 1? You can reverse out of the forward swap, but this will result in a less than perfect match of the hedge and the exposure. You cannot match a five-year note issued on August 1 with a five-year swap that starts a month and a half later. We saw the same issue with futures hedges in Chapter 7. The time gap cannot be addressed using a forward swap or a Treasury lock. However, the gap can be bridged if you bought an *American swaption*, which can be exercised at any time during the option period. That way, on August 1 the hedge is a five-year swap valued that day.

MATURING DEBT

Forward swaps and swaptions can be used to hedge debt to be issued much further in the future. If you think interest rates are near bottom, you may not want to wait two years for existing notes to mature before fixing a rate on new debt. Forward swaps and swaptions can start as far ahead as 10 years from today. If the company is planning to fund on a floating rate basis, it will want to analyze a forward cap, as well as a forward swap, plus the combinations discussed in Chapter 9.

CALLABLE DEBT

Over the years, many companies have funded themselves in the public markets by issuing notes and bonds they could retire, or *call*, after a number of years. They feel that the premium paid to investors for the call privilege is small relative to the flexibility it gives their corporate financing program.

NEW NOTE ISSUE

Callable notes used together with swaptions give companies another avenue to consider when pricing debt alternatives. The alternatives we looked at earlier were a bank loan and a swap to pay fixed and receive floating and a fixed rate note issue.

The premise behind callable notes and swaptions is that the premium paid to investors for the call feature of the notes is less than the premium earned by selling a similar call feature in the derivatives market. Let's say you issue a five-year note callable in the second year. At the same time, you sell to a bank the right to ask you to pay a fixed rate for three years, starting at the end of the second year. And you receive a premium from the bank for selling the swaption. Your alternatives are:

Bank Loan and Swap	
Loan:	Libor + 0.30%
Swap:	8.90%
Cost of funds:	9.20%
Issue Fixed Rate Note	
Note rate:	9.15%
Cost of funds:	9.15%
Issue Callable Note and Sell Swaption	
Callable note rate:	9.21%
Swaption premium (0.75%):	(0.19%)
(Swap rate of 8.90%):	
Cost of funds:	9.02%

The third alternative appears to be less expensive than issuing a fixed rate note (a difference of $650,000 over five years). But it is not that simple, since the bank owns an option it can exercise when the time is right. You need to analyze when the bank is likely to exercise its option and what the effect will be. At the end of two years, if interest rates have increased, the bank will not be interested in exercising the option to receive a fixed rate of 8.90 percent for the subsequent three years. You will keep the note outstanding.

If interest rates have decreased, the bank will be interested in exercising its right under the swaption. The bank will elect to receive the fixed rate of 8.90 percent and pay you Libor. You are now in the position of having issued a fixed rate note *and* paying a fixed rate on the swap. You call the note and borrow from the bank at Libor plus 0.30 percent. Your situation is:

Loan:	Libor + 0.30%	
Swap:	8.90%	
Swaption premium:	(0.19%)	
Cost of funds:	9.01%	— for the last three years

You end up paying an effective rate of 9.01 percent for the last three years of funding. The analysis shows that you are indifferent to the bank exercising its option. By buying an option in the investor market and selling the same option in the derivatives market, you earned 13 basis points. And you constructed a swaption in which the cost of funds remains nearly constant.

EXISTING CALLABLE NOTES

An extension of this strategy is often employed when companies believe that rates are at the bottom of the interest rate cycle. Selling a swaption also can be employed with existing callable notes. Premium income is earned today, thereby reducing funding costs. Selling swaptions against callable notes is referred to as *monetizing the value of the call.* The analysis of the appropriateness of selling a swaption against existing debt is the same as for new debt.

REDUCING COST, INCREASING FLEXIBILITY

In a steep yield curve environment, fixing the cost of floating rate debt can represent a significant step up from short term rates. A 2 percent difference between three-month and seven-year rates occurred in the early 1990s. One way you can lower the cost of a swap is by selling to a bank the right to terminate the swap agreement on a predetermined date prior to maturity. If a standard seven-year swap is 8 percent, the rate for a seven-year swap where you pay the fixed rate *and* agree to sell the bank the right to cancel the swap at the end of the fifth year is 7.60 percent. Or, you can arrange with the bank to take the premium of 2.12 percent right away and pay a rate of 8 percent on the swap.

The bank's view of this transaction is that it is receiving 8 percent on a swap and has the right to get out of the deal at the end of five years. If rates for the last two years are greater than 8 percent, the bank will cancel the swap. This is, of course, precisely the time you would like to be paying a fixed rate. If the bank cancels the swap, your alternatives are to hedge again at the prevailing market rates via another swap or cap, or to borrow unhedged for the last two years.

In assessing strategies, you need to make an estimate of what two-year rates will be five years from today, how important the amount of the swap is in relation to its overall funding portfolio, and what rate level would be unacceptable, considering the lower swap rate you are receiving for the first five years. By calculating the return from investing the premium, you can figure the break-even rate in years six and seven. In our example, you could afford to pay 9.55 percent and not be worse off than if you had entered into a standard swap and paid 8 percent.

In another interest rate environment, you may want to buy the right to extend the fixed rate you have on the swap. For this you will pay a fee, either a higher swap coupon or a premium. Then, if interest rates are higher at the end of five years, you can extend the swap. If rates are lower than the swap coupon, you will not extend.

SWAPTION TERMINOLOGY

Swaptions have attracted a number of different names. It is therefore important to be clear about the kind of transaction you want to enter into. Table 11.1 lists the types of transactions and the names used for them.

Table 11.1 Types of Options on Swaps

Right of the Buyer	Names
To receive the fixed rate on a swap	Swaption Call swaption
To pay the fixed rate on a swap	Swaption Put swaption Contingent swap
To extend the fixed rate on the swap	Callable swap Extendible swap
To terminate the swap	Puttable swap Cancelable swap

Source: Terminology from Burghardt, Belton, Lane, Luce, McVey, *Eurodollar Futures and Options,* Chicago, Probus Publishing Company, 1991, p. 229 and *Derivatives Strategy,* Vol. 3, No. 10/11, July 18,1994, p. 40.

In Chapter 9, we looked at the different combinations of caps and floors and how they were combined into collars and corridors and used with swaps to create participating hedges. You can put together the same combinations with swaptions and forward swaps.

PRICING

The principles for pricing forward swaps are the same as for pricing any forward rate. The formula is the same as used in Chapter 6. The price of the forward swap will be a combination of (1) the swap rate for the period from today until the swap starts, and (2) the swap rate for the period from today until the swap ends. For example, if you want to hedge an investment planned to start two years from now and running for three years thereafter, you would use the two-year offered rate and the five-year bid rate. If the two-year swap were quoted at 5.70 percent to 5.74 percent and the five-year quote were 6.50 percent to 6.54 percent, then the fixed rate you would receive for three years, two years from today, would be 6.29 percent.[1]

Options on swaps are sensitive to the same variables as caps. But, whereas a cap features a series of increasingly long option periods on short term money, generally three months, swaptions feature a single option period on long term money. For example, the last caplet in a five-year cap against three-month Libor has an option period of 57 months on a three-month instrument. A swaption of the same tenor may feature a two-year option on a three-year swap. As a result, swaption premiums are a function of the term of the swap, intrinsic value of the swap as measured against the forward swap, volatility of the swap rate, and whether the swaption is American or European.

The volatility numbers used for swaptions, as well as caps and floors, are derived from measurements of how the relevant instruments are currently being priced in the market. By looking at cap and swaption premiums paid and received in the market and by knowing the relevant interest rates, you can apply an option pricing model and derive the volatilities implied by these premiums. The volatilities for caps, floors, and swaptions are regularly published by Bloomberg, Reuters, and Telerate data services. Generally, the volatilities for caps and floors are greater than for swaptions because short term rates tend to move more than long term rates.

NOTE

1. The calculation of the forward swap rate two years forward, for three years is:

$$\frac{(1 + .065 \times 5)}{(1 + .0574 \times 2)} - 1 \times 1/3 = 6.29\%$$

SOURCES

Sources on the uses of swaptions for this chapter include:

Laurie S. Goodman, "The Use of Interest Rate Swaps in Managing Corporate Liabilities," in Robert J. Schwartz and Clifford W. Smith, Jr., ed., *Advanced Strategies in Financial Risk Management,* New York, New York, Institute of Finance, 1993, pp. 103-127.

Jeffrey Pearsall and Townsend Walker, "Understanding Swaptions: Strategies for Liability Management," unpublished monograph, 1993.

CHAPTER 12

Derivative Credit Risk

Used appropriately, derivatives insure against sudden declines in your company's value and reduce the volatility of its cash flow. Before using derivatives, you should understand the credit risk introduced by these transactions. Bankers care about credit risk because if they have loaned a company $50 million and the company now wants to enter into a swap for that amount to fix its interest payments, the bank wants to know if its exposure is now $52 million, $60 million, or $75 million. A company treasurer also cares about credit risk. If the bank does not perform, losses are not insured by the Federal Deposit Insurance Corporation (FDIC). The risk is two-sided; both the company and the bank accept the risk that the other party may not perform. The credit risk for derivatives is harder to assess than with loans, because with loans a principal amount is outstanding. Derivatives do not give the credit analyst the same convenient handle.

In coming to grips with the credit risk of derivatives, the first task is to understand what the company and the bank obligations are in each type of derivatives transaction. To do this we'll first look at a company as a borrower, and then at a company as an investor, because the types of transactions they typically do are different. Second, we'll look at how to estimate the amount of credit risk in swaps. Third, we'll look at what measures can be taken to reduce credit risk if it is higher than desired. Finally we'll look at how to manage credit problems with companies with whom you have a derivatives transaction. The last section looks at the standard agreement that is used for derivatives transactions.

COMPANY AS BORROWER

We'll first consider the case of a company that would buy a cap or pay fixed rate on a swap. Table 12.1 shows the obligations the bank and the company have to one another. A loan is included in the comparison because it is familiar to both bankers and company treasurers.

From the bank's point of view, if the company buys a cap, the credit exposure only lasts until the premium is paid, two days from the date of the transaction. With a swap, the credit exposure lasts until the swap matures. As short term rates rise, the company's obligation decreases, and when short term rates are higher than the fixed rate, the company has no obligation to the bank. The bank has the obligation to pay the company. As interest rates fall, however, the company's credit exposure rises.

Table 12.1 Swap and Cap Obligations—Borrower and Bank

	Loan		Swap		Cap	
Time (days)	**Borrower**	**Bank**	**Borrower**	**Bank**	**Borrower**	**Bank**
2		Fund loan			Pay premium	
90	Pay floating interest		Pay, if fixed is greater than floating rate	Pay, if floating is greater than fixed rate		Pay, if floating is greater than cap rate
180	Pay floating interest		Pay, if fixed is greater than floating rate	Pay, if floating is greater than fixed rate		Pay, if floating is greater than cap rate
1826	Pay floating interest and principal		Pay, if fixed is greater than floating rate	Pay, if floating is greater than fixed rate		Pay, if floating is greater than cap rate

Note: This framework and that in Table 12.2 were developed in 1993 by John Doble and the author for a workshop on foreign exchange and derivative credit risk.

COMPANY AS INVESTOR

Investors have several basic derivative alternatives: (1) receive a fixed rate on a swap, (2) buy a floor, or (3) if floor premiums seem expensive, sell a cap to offset the cost of the floor. In Chapter 9, we looked at companies with debt buying a cap and selling a floor, to form a collar. This is the same principle in reverse—an investor collar. Table 12.2 shows the company and bank obligations for this set of transactions.

When short term rates rise higher than the fixed rate on the swap and the cap, the company becomes obligated to the bank. This credit exposure rises when interest rates rise; it falls when interest rates fall.

ESTIMATING THE AMOUNT OF DERIVATIVE CREDIT RISK

It takes two events, happening at the same time, to cause a credit problem with a derivatives transaction: market interest rates move against the derivatives transaction *and* the company defaults. At the start of a transaction, each party wants to know what the potential amount of the loss will be if the other party defaults. This section looks at a way of estimating this amount.

Let's look at a swap in terms of payments and rates. As of today, we know the number of payments at risk will decrease as time goes by. Rates, however, are less predictable the further out we look. Therefore, it is convenient to break the exposure into those two elements. First, the payment risk decreases as time goes on, simply because there are fewer future payments to be made. Second, rate risk increases as we look into the future.

To generate a forecast on future rates, we can use the binomial model or Monte Carlo simulation discussed in Chapter 3. David Rowe[1] suggests an alternative that can provide a realistic assessment within a trading time frame.

Assume that interest rates change from day to day by a random amount (proportional to the rate on the previous day), and that expected future rates are described by today's forward rates. Select a volatility level on the basis of past market behavior. The resulting rate distributions are similar to the patterns observed with the binomial model and Monte Carlo simulation. Illustration 12.1

Table 12.2 Swap, Floor, and Cap Obligations—Investor and Bank

	Swap		Floor		Cap	
Time (days)	**Investor**	**Bank**	**Investor**	**Bank**	**Investor**	**Bank**
2			Pay premium			Pay premium
90	Pay, if floating is greater than fixed rate	Pay, if fixed is greater than floating rate		Pay, if floating is lower than floor rate	Pay, if floating is higher than cap rate	
180	Pay, if floating is greater than fixed rate	Pay, if fixed is greater than floating rate		Pay, if floating is lower than floor rate	Pay, if floating is higher than cap rate	
1826	Pay, if floating is greater than fixed rate	Pay, if fixed is greater than floating rate		Pay, if floating is lower than floor rate	Pay, if floating is higher than cap rate	

shows the distribution of future interest rates over different periods of time.

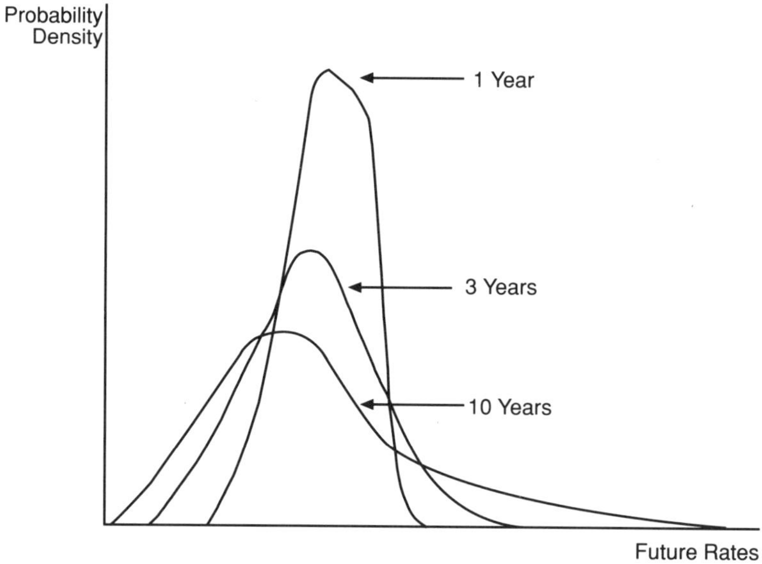

Illustration 12.1 Probability Distributions for Future Interest Rates

Source: Adapted from David Rowe, "Curves of Confidence," *RISK*, Vol. 6, No. 11, November 1993, pp. 52-56.

It is standard in the derivatives industry to use a range of rates for estimating exposure that includes 95 percent of the possibilities, which is two standard deviations. Ten years in the future, that range is 2.24 percent to 13.19 percent.

The combination of time and rate movement produces an exposure profile like that shown in Illustration 12.2. A time profile of exposure is more representative of the risk to the bank than a single number. For a loan, the risk is usually captured by the amount outstanding. But, a single number for derivatives risk would overestimate or underestimate the situation. In addition, it would hide the period of peak exposure.

Exposure is measured as positive if rates have moved away from the protection feature provided by the swap. The borrower protects against a rise in rates by paying the fixed rate, so a fall in interest rates creates positive exposure. The investor protects against a fall in rates by receiving the fixed rate, so a rise in interest rates creates positive exposure.

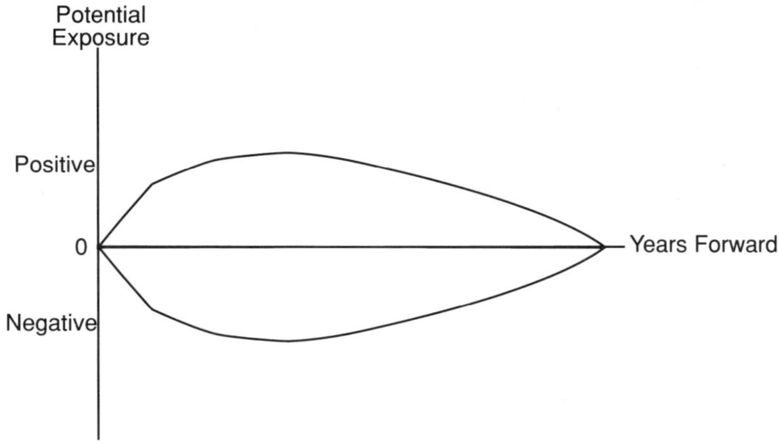

Illustration 12.2 Swap Exposure Over Time

To generate the points on the curve, we look at the payment dates and the range of interest rates estimated for each of those dates, then calculate the potential credit exposure. For example, there is a range of rates around the six-month payment date, there is another range of rates around the 12-month payment date, and so on. The upper portion of the curve shows the region where the bank is exposed to the company. The lower portion shows the profile of the company's exposure to the bank. The two sides will not necessarily be symmetrical if the rate estimating procedure uses forward rates as expected future rates. If the slope of the forward curve is positive, the exposure profile for a swap where the company pays the fixed rate will have less amplitude than where the company receives the fixed rate.

This procedure is followed to assess the credit commitment a bank makes when it considers entering into a swap transaction with a company. Over the life of the transaction, the credit exposure needs to be continually monitored because interest rates change, the forward curve shifts, and volatility of interest rates changes. Six months into the transaction, interest rates will certainly have changed. If rates went down from the time the borrower entered into its swap, the swap has less value. To capture the total exposure the bank has to the company, add the current exposure to the potential exposure to arrive at the total risk. Illustration 12.3 shows a new exposure diagram for the company. Note that the exposure now starts at a positive level, not at zero as shown in Illustration 12.2.

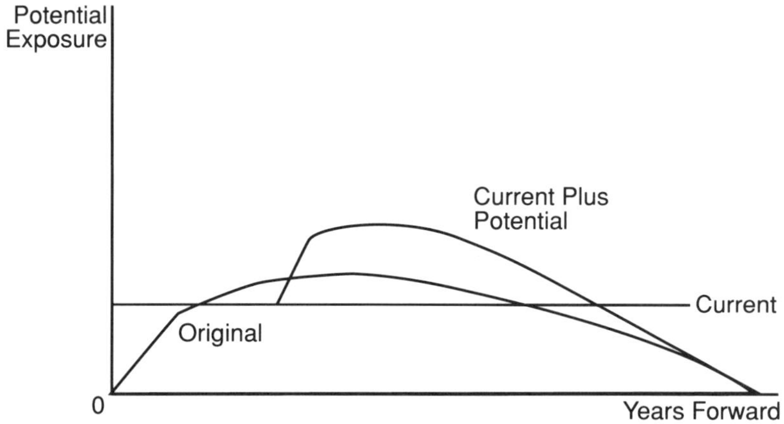

Illustration 12.3 Current Plus Potential Exposure

One issue bankers face is how to aggregate credit exposure on a swap to credit exposure of a loan to the same company. If the company defaults on all payments, the bank will have a loss on the loan, and *possibly* on the swap. It is equally clear that if the company is using swaps to hedge interest rate exposure, it is less likely to run into financial difficulty and default on its payments. Adding swap and loan exposure, therefore, does not provide the answer.

The key to assessing a company's credit exposure is to recognize that it has more than one dimension. The distinction is between direct exposure and contingent exposure. Direct exposure includes interest and principal owed on a loan and the current positive exposure on the swap. These elements can be added together. Contingent exposure includes performance under letters of credit and potential swap exposure. When speaking about a company's exposure, a banker should think in terms of the two dimensions and not add them together.

MEASURES TO REDUCE RISK

We now look at the alternatives available to a bank if it is uncomfortable with the risk generated by a swap, but still wants to help the other party hedge its exposure. We'll start with the exposure shown in Illustration 12.4 and then show how different measures alter it.

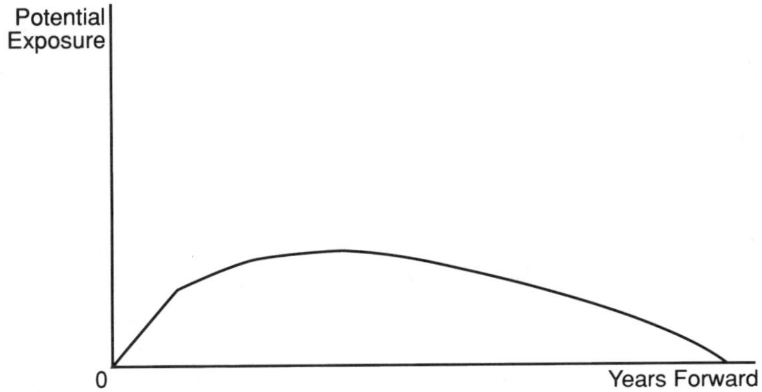

Illustration 12.4 Exposure to Fixed Rate Payer

The measures are:

- reduce the maturity of the proposed swap
- agree to a mutual put after three years
- ask the other party to post collateral
- arrange credit triggers
- change the coupon on the swap
- sell the company a cap

REDUCE THE MATURITY OF THE SWAP

Reducing the maturity of the swap shortens both the length of time the bank is exposed to the company and lowers the maximum point of exposure. (See Illustration 12.5.)

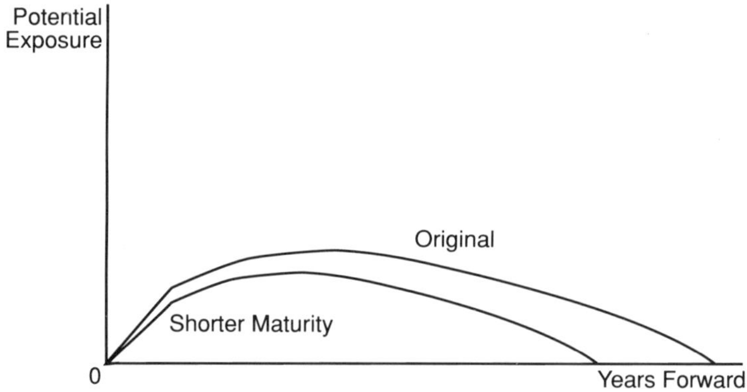

Illustration 12.5 Reduction of Exposure by Reduction of Maturity

AGREE TO A MUTUAL PUT

A mutual put enables either side of the transaction to terminate the swap agreement at a specified point in the future, for example, three years into a five-year trade. In the event of termination, the parties agree on the value of the swap, and cash is paid out to the party for whom the termination would cause a loss. For example, a company has a five-year swap at 7 percent fixed. After three years, rates have gone up and two-year swaps are now 9 percent. If the mutual put provision is activated, the company would receive a cash payment from the bank. Illustration 12.6 shows how the mutual put shortens the tenor of the exposure but does not lower the maximum point of the exposure.

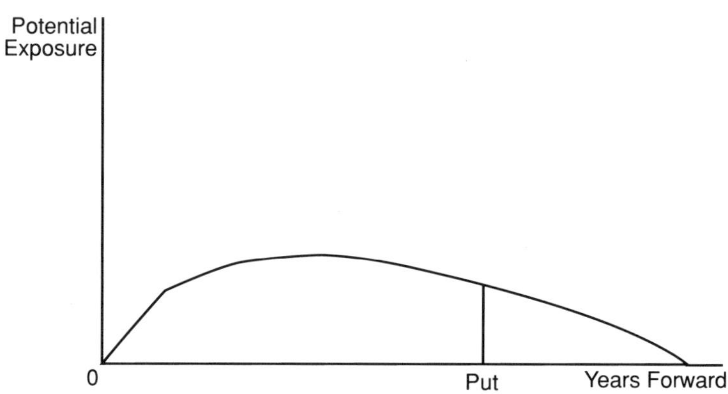

Illustration 12.6 Mutual Put

POST COLLATERAL

The bank can request that a company put up collateral against an unfavorable movement in interest rates. Collateral is handled in several different ways.

Ex post: Following the calculation of the value of the swap, often termed *mark to market*, the company is obligated to post cash or acceptable securities equal to the mark to market if rates have moved and the bank's exposure has increased. If the company is unable or unwilling to post collateral, the bank is authorized to terminate the transaction. If it terminates the transaction, the bank has a loss in the amount of the mark to market.

Ex post with a cushion: Rather than bother with small collateral calls, the company and the bank agree to a threshold amount; when the mark to market exceeds it, the right to collateral is triggered. This method, and the previous one, provide credit protection after the bank is actually exposed. The next method protects the bank before the exposure has happened.

A priori: In this case, the bank requires the company to post an initial margin as a buffer against future adverse rate movements. More collateral is added when the bank's exposure increases above the initial level.

Illustration 12.7 shows how collateral will reduce both the amplitude of the exposure and its tenor.

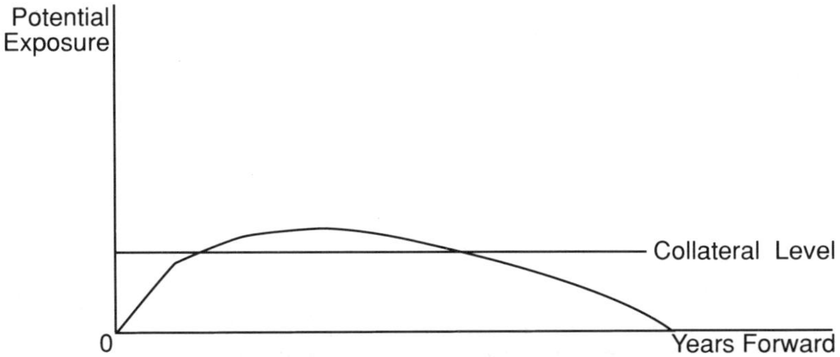

Illustration 12.7 Collateral

ARRANGE A CREDIT TRIGGER

A credit trigger gives a company the right to obtain credit protection if its counterparty becomes financially weaker sometime during the life of the swap. Usually the mechanism is triggered by a rating agency downgrade. A credit trigger can be designed to operate a couple of ways: (1) the swap is terminated and a payment made, depending on which way rates have moved; or (2) the downgraded party puts up collateral. The first way looks like a mutual put; the second way looks like a collateral call.

CHANGE THE COUPON

When the current level of swap coupons is very different from the level on the original deal, the coupon is changed and a payment is made. A significant change in rates can create large actual exposure for one of the parties to the transaction. The actual exposure is eliminated by the payment and change in the coupon. However, there is still potential exposure.

SELL A CAP

If the bank is unwilling to accept any exposure from a company, yet wants to help it hedge its exposure to floating rate loans, the bank can sell the company a cap. The exposure lasts for only two days. If necessary, the company can deposit the cap premium prior to executing the transaction.

MANAGING CREDIT PROBLEMS

One of the bank's customers is in financial difficulty. The bank is a counterparty on a swap with the company. The company is paying a fixed rate on the swap. The bank has a positive exposure of $1 million to the company on the swap. Buyouts, assignments, and buying protection are measures used to manage the bank's situation.

BUYOUTS

To close out the swap would cost $1 million. The bank and the company might be willing to end the transaction for a smaller amount. The nature of the settlement will depend on the level of the bank's discomfort, its assessment of what it might realize subsequently, the cash position of the company, and its willingness to reach an agreement.

ASSIGNMENTS

Different banks have different levels of comfort with the same company. A deal might be struck with another bank to take over the transaction. This might be done without a loss, or, if the bank is required to compromise, it might be less than the company would require in a buyout.

PROTECTION

To protect itself from further credit exposure, the bank can buy protection. Its current exposure to the customer will not diminish unless interest rates go up. In this situation, exposure increases as interest rates fall. If the bank thinks rates will continue to fall, it has a number of alternatives to protect itself: enter into a swap to receive a fixed rate, buy a swaption that gives it the right to receive a fixed rate, or buy a floor.

DERIVATIVE AGREEMENT

The standard agreement for derivative transactions is the 1992 ISDA (International Swaps and Derivatives Association) Master Agreement. Since the early 1980s, the Association has labored to establish legal and regulatory standards for derivative transactions. The ISDA Master is unquestionably the standard in the United States and for all cross-border transactions in the world. If you are thinking about entering into a derivatives transaction, you should read the ISDA Master Agreement and the relevant portions of *1991 ISDA Definitions* and *User's Guide to the 1992 ISDA Master Agreements*, 1993 Edition.[2] The Master Agreement should be signed before entering into a transaction because it gives you a considerable amount of protection if your counterparty cannot meet its obligations, and it details the procedures for settling a transaction that has been interrupted in the middle. Among other things, the Master Agreement has the following features: it defines the events of default and events of termination; it provides for a cross-default on any other obligations with the counterparty; it describes the procedures for determining the current values of terminated transactions; and on termination, it allows you to net the amounts you owe against the amounts your counterparty owes you on the terminated derivatives transactions (swaps, caps, collars, swaptions, FRAs, and others).

While negotiating a Master Agreement with prospective counterparties, you should keep a few things in mind.

- If you are going to enter into only U.S. dollar-denominated transactions, you can use the simpler of the two Master Agreements—the single currency agreement. It is shorter and less complex than the agreement designed to cover cross-border, multicurrency transactions.
- If you are going to enter into derivatives transactions with a bank, you need to put language in the Master Agreement to cover the possibility that the bank becomes insolvent. The standard Agreement covers only counterparties that are subject to the Bankruptcy Code.
- If you are going to enter into swaps only with banks or companies headquartered in the United States, you can eliminate all of the wording covering withholding taxes.
- If you are entering into a long term derivatives transaction, you should consider inserting appropriate collateral provisions in the Agreement. The fortunes of your counterparty can change over time.
- If you are concerned about defaults resulting from payment errors, be sure to set a reasonable amount for payment defaults. The standard agreement triggers defaults for small amounts of money.
- If your relationship with your potential derivatives counterparty includes loans, deposits, and foreign exchange contracts, you can include a provision to net all of the obligations in the event of a default.[3]

Derivatives transactions, particularly if documented by an ISDA Master Agreement, have a special place in the U.S. Bankruptcy Code, as amended in 1990, and in the regulations governing the insolvency of financial institutions as defined in the Financial Institutions Reform, Recovery, and Enforcement Act of 1989 (FIRREA), which amended the Federal Deposit Insurance Act (FDIA). The effects of the 1990 amendment to the Bankruptcy Code are to allow the nonbankrupt party to exercise contractual rights to terminate derivatives agreements following a bankruptcy filing and to use collateral held to satisfy any amounts due from the bankrupt party. The amendment also explicitly recognizes the right to look to all the derivatives contracts with a counterparty and net the payments and termination values. And, the amended Code protects transfers made under a derivatives agreement that take place within 90 days of the time bankruptcy was filed. Normally, a bankruptcy trustee has the power to void payments and other transfers within the 90-day window.[4]

FIRREA applies to federally insured and chartered financial institutions and generally follows the logic of the bankruptcy code. There are, however, some important differences, because the insolvency of a financial institution is not handled the same way as the bankruptcy of a company. FIRREA makes the distinction between a conservator and receiver. The appointment of the FDIC as conservator for an insolvent institution means it will continue to operate. There is no reason, therefore, to declare a default and seek remedies under the Master Agreement. You can declare a default only if the FDIC subsequently fails to comply with the terms of the Master Agreement.

When a failed institution is placed in receivership by the FDIC, it is liquidated and its assets and obligations are transferred to another financial institution (either existing or newly organized). You can only declare a default and seek remedies under the Master Agreement after waiting 24 hours to see if the derivatives contracts have been transferred.

Overriding these provisions is the power of the FDIC as conservator or receiver to "repudiate" agreements if it determines that the agreement is burdensome and repudiation would make administration of the failed institution's affairs more orderly. However, the FDIA has a general rule that you can recover damages if an agreement is repudiated.[5]

This section provided a brief overview of the legal aspects of derivatives and highlighted the principal issues. Before entering into a derivatives transaction, be sure you understand the agreements and the implications of them. Consult legal counsel.

NOTES

1. The basic assumptions are that there is a flat yield curve, all maturities are 6 percent, and annual volatility is 14 percent.

2. These documents are available from the International Swap and Derivatives Association, 1270 Avenue of the Americas, Rockefeller Center, Suite 2118, New York, NY 10020. They should also be available from swap dealers with whom you intend to do business.

3. Tina Auyter, "Don't Sign That Swap Contract Until You Read This Article," *Derivatives Strategy*, Vol 1, No. 1, pp. 42-44.

4. Cravath, Swaine & Moore, "U.S. Bankruptcy Code Amendments for Swap Transactions," memorandum, June 28, 1990.

5. Walter Eccard and Seth Grosshandler, "Qualified Financial Contracts with FDIC-Insured Banks and Thrifts," *The Review of Banking and Financial Services,* Vol. 7, No. 7, April 10,1991, pp. 49-58.

CHAPTER 13

How Interest Rate Exposure Occurs in Banks

For the first 12 chapters, we focused on the exposures faced by companies and the derivatives solutions to those exposures. This and the following chapter focus on some of the special interest rate exposure problems faced by banks. Company treasurers can skip to Chapter 15. The reason for a focus on banks is that interest rate exposure is much more important to them than it is to most companies. For companies, interest rate risk is something to be managed while they go about their main business of making cars, computers, or soap. For banks, interest rate risk is central to the business; managing it successfully is how banks make money.

In this chapter, we'll identify the rate indices used for a bank's principal assets and liabilities. Then we'll see how mismatches among the indices occur, and how embedded options in bank assets and liabilities affect interest margins. The following section looks at other asset/liability management issues that generate interest rate exposure that can be addressed with derivatives. The final section examines how interest rate risk is measured in banks.

RATE INDICES

Banks are very specific about the rate index involved in their exposure. It is not simply a matter of fixed versus floating rate exposures. Most banks have at least a dozen or so different rate indices attached to their assets and liabilities. This is a reflection of the different sources from which they draw their funds and the customization of lending rates to attract borrowers. This section tries to distill the number of indices down to their basic features. We'll look at asset and liability rate indices.

ASSETS

Commercial loan assets are generally priced on the basis of prime or Libor.

Mortgages are based on Treasury rates, both fixed and floating; certificate of deposit (CD) rates; Libor; and the 11th District Cost of Funds Index (COFI).

Auto loans are generally priced as a spread over the average life treasury.

Most credit card rates are administratively set on the basis of the market niche the bank is looking for. There is no clear relation, except for some prime-based cards, to a rate index.

Securities in the investment portfolio carry short and long term Treasury rates, government agency rates, asset-backed security rates, and mortgage-backed security rates. The latter three are generally priced as a spread over treasuries.

LIABILITIES

Fed Funds are based on the Fed Funds rate.

Money market demand accounts (MMDAs) are not closely tied to another rate index. They are set largely in response to local market conditions—what the bank next door is paying.

Certificates of deposit are priced on the basis of Treasury bills and local market conditions.

Eurodollar deposits are based on Libor.

Longer term deposits and bank notes are generally priced as a spread over Treasury notes.

MISMATCHES

On the face of it, there should not be that much of a problem matching assets and liabilities. Table 13.1 shows that four of the seven indices for assets and liabilities are the same.

Table 13.1 Pricing of Assets and Liabilities

Asset Pricing	Liability Pricing
Treasuries, short term	Treasuries, short term
Treasuries, long term	Treasuries, long term
Libor, various maturities	Libor, various maturities
CDs	CDs
Prime	Fed Funds
COFI	Competition for deposits
Competition for loans	

In the nature of banking, however, depositors and borrowers have different appetites and so create mismatches for a bank. There are mismatches in quantity, maturity, and rate indices. Some indices are averages of past rates (lagging indices), and some assets and liabilities contain embedded options.

QUANTITY

Assets and liabilities that share the same rate index are not necessarily available to a bank in the quantity needed. You may be very successful in making Libor-based loans, but your ability to attract Libor deposits may be limited. You will have to fund the Libor loans with liabilities based on another index, thereby introducing interest rate exposure. The exposure may result from a difference in the frequency with which two indices reset, or the two rate indices may be influenced by different events. For example, the Fed Funds rate is set by the Federal Reserve; Libor, however, depends on the Funds rate, the international supply and demand for short term deposits, and expectations of what is going to happen in the short term money market.

MATURITY

Assets and liabilities that share the same rate index are not necessarily available to a bank in the same maturities. You may be able to match the amount of Libor loans and deposits, but the customers are looking for six-month loans and you can attract only one-month deposits. The two rates do not have a constant spread between them. The result of this mismatch is interest rate exposure. Illustration 13.1 shows the minimum and maximum spread between the two rates from 1975 to 1994.

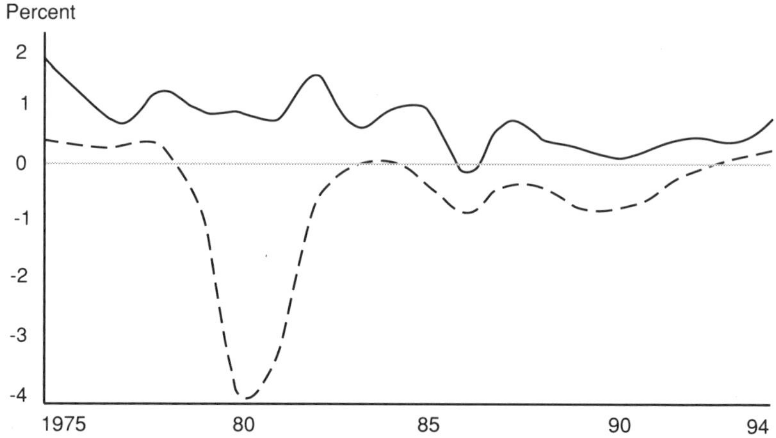

Illustration 13.1 Spread—Six-Month Minus One-Month Libor, Minimum and Maximum

Source: Data from V.K. Ranganathan, *Interest Rate Trends & Comparisons,* New York, Bank of America, 1995, p. 38.

RATE INDICES

Given the variety of indices between the asset and liability sides of the balance sheet, it is inevitable that funds priced off one index will be used to fund assets priced off of another. Up to now, we have classified financial instruments as fixed or floating, and we have assumed that a floating rate asset and a liability would offset one another. Yet, many of the short term floating rate indices do not move together in a systematic fashion. This movement is termed *basis risk*. It means that you cannot depend on a stable lending spread and are exposed to interest rate risk. Illustration 13.2 shows the difficulty of funding prime loans at a predictable margin. Notice that the spread between prime and Libor and prime and Fed Funds moved considerably between 1975 and 1994.

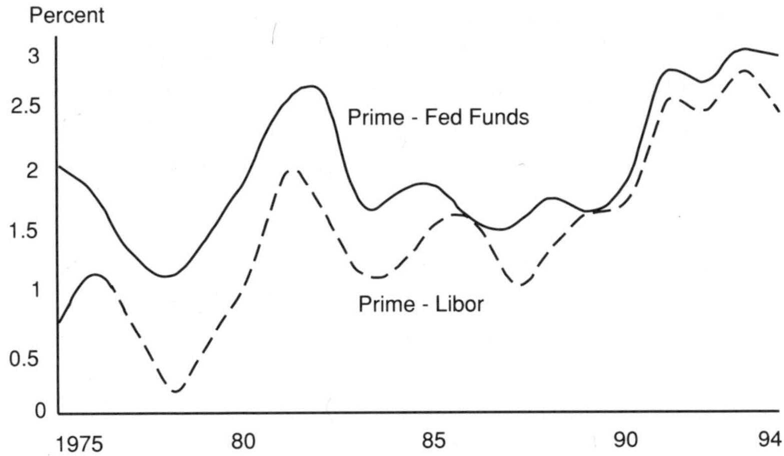

Illustration 13.2 Spread between Prime and Libor and Prime and Fed Funds

Source: Ibid., pp. 201, 211.

LAGGING INDICES

Mortgage rates often are based on past rates rather than current rates. The COFI index is based on past rates and on a combination of short and long term rates. It is not possible to fund it precisely from a single source. In addition, the index lags behind when interest rates are rising, leading to a compression of margins. The benefit is that it also lags behind when rates are falling. Even mortgage rates based on your bank's own CD are often an average of previous months' rates rather than current rates. It is not possible for the funding side to match the repricing characteristics of the mortgage portfolio with this structure.

EMBEDDED OPTIONS

When you lend to their customers on an installment basis—mortgages, auto loans, or equipment loans—you usually give the customer the right to repay the loan in full at any time without a penalty. We call it "embedded" because it is part of the mortgage; it is not a separate transaction. You have effectively sold the customer an American option to cancel, like the swaption we described in Chapter 11. In that instance, an explicit premium is charged for the option. With installment loans, it is not. The same is true of MMDAs: the customer has the option to withdraw funds at any time without penalty. The difference between the options sold to an individual company and those sold to a group of customers is that an individual company will act more predictably than retail customers. As a banker, you can predict more accurately when a company will exercise its option than you can predict when retail customers will exercise theirs.

In the early 1990s, institutions that held fixed rate mortgages and mortgage-backed securities were hit hard as rates fell. Homeowners repaid and refinanced at a lower rate. The mortgage with a final maturity of 30 years, and an average life of seven years, effectively repriced in two years. Floating rate mortgage portfolios scheduled to reprice yearly behaved as if they were repricing monthly. As rates rise, the pace of refinancing slows down and the average life of the mortgage becomes longer, and repricing is less frequent. This phenomenon affects not only the mortgages in the loan portfolio, but also the mortgage-backed securities in the investment portfolio. There are not any natural funding sources that match this behavior; the result is interest rate exposure.

The behavior of MMDAs is also affected by interest rates. As interest rates fall, depositors begin to look for higher returns; they withdraw their money and place it in stock and bond mutual funds. So, the bank is losing its least expensive source of funds when loan rates are falling and the "fixed rate" portfolios are repricing. In addition, in low interest rate environments, MMDA rates and other retail deposit rates move down more slowly than loan rates. This results in a compression of lending margins.

While the exposure of the mortgage portfolio and MMDAs results largely from rate movement, the exposure of the auto loan portfolio is affected more by the state of the economy. When the economy is strong, new cars are bought, old car loans are paid off, and new car loans are taken out. The fixed rate auto loan portfolio reprices at current rates.

Consumers who prepay their loans or withdraw their deposits do not do so in a fashion that can be neatly modeled. Homeowners who repay their loans do not look at the absolute rate at which they can refinance, but rather at the difference between that and their current rate. Their behavior depends not only on the current rate level but on rates in the past. And their behavior depends on what others are doing; refinancing is cumulative. This presents a serious challenge to managing the rate risk of mortgage loan and mortgage-backed securities portfolios.

OTHER ASSET/LIABILITY MANAGEMENT ISSUES

Banks often go through cycles where loan demand does not keep up with the ability to gather deposits. But they are reluctant to turn away deposits since they are one of the prime avenues for selling other banking services. This makes it difficult to redeploy the deposits and earn a meaningful spread on them. Investing in long term securities creates an interest rate exposure and may pose liquidity concerns.

The ability to buy and sell securities in the investment portfolio is restricted by the Office of the Comptroller of the Currency's (OCC) regulations. If you rebalance the portion of the portfolio that has been designated "hold to maturity," you risk losing accrual accounting treatment on it. As interest rates and interest rate expectations change, the maturity of the portfolio may become too long, a gap may develop in the maturity ladder of the portfolio, and its value and earnings ability will shrink as the cost of funding it rises.

MEASURING INTEREST RATE RISK

There are several ways to measure the interest rate risk of banks: gap, dynamic gap, duration gap, funds allocation, simulation, market value, and the OCC's method for risk-based capital. We looked at gap and dynamic gap in a corporate context in Chapter 3. The principles are the same for banks.

DURATION GAP

One of the motivations for the duration gap measure is that the maturity buckets rarely show a consistent pattern of asset or liability sensitivity. The 3- to 6-month bucket shows the bank will gain if rates go up, the 6- to 12-month bucket shows it will lose if rates go up, the 1- to 2-year bucket shows it will gain if rates go up, and so on. It is not easy to hedge that kind of exposure. It may not be necessary, however, to hedge every exposure; it may be enough to ensure that the magnitude and timing of the liability cash flows match the magnitude and timing of the asset cash flows on average. A way to arrive at this average is to calculate the duration of the bank's assets and the duration of its liabilities. The net of the two numbers is your bank's exposure to interest rate movements.

FUNDS ALLOCATION

The funds allocation approach ranks assets and liabilities and equity by the frequency with which their rates changes. Common equity is at the least frequent end of the liability/equity spectrum. Fed Funds purchased are at the most frequent end. Assets on the least frequent end of the spectrum are the bank building and furniture; on the most frequent end, Fed Funds sold. The allocation procedure is to fund fixed assets first, then 30-year loans, then five-year loans, then one-year loans, and so on. The procedure starts with equity, then long term liabilities, medium term liabilities, and so on. For example, the funding for prime rate, commercial loan portfolios may be six-month CDs. When all of the six-month CDs have been used, three-month CDs are used, and then Eurodollar deposits. The result is a clear picture, on the basis of the frequency of rate change, of the sectors of the balance sheet where the bank does, or does not, have interest rate exposure.

SIMULATION MODELS

Simulation models make assumptions about the future volume and mix of loans and the family of future interest rates (Fed Funds, three-month Libor, prime, five-year Treasuries, etc.). Equations are the heart of simulation models. They generally are derived from historical information that relates external variables to the behavior of the balance sheet and income statement. Simulation models are not easy to use correctly; their virtue is that they allow your bank to examine systematically what may happen in the future.

MARKET VALUE

The market value approach is based on the premise that the bank with the highest market value will have the highest future earnings potential. Market value is the risk-adjusted value of future income streams. First, future cash flows, without option characteristics, are discounted at current market rates. Those asset and liability items that have embedded options are adjusted to account for the option behavior in different interest rate scenarios. Then, to test the interest rate sensitivity of your bank, the individual discount rates are moved up and down. The result is the change in the current market value of your bank.

OCC

The OCC is approaching interest rate risk on the basis of what a change in interest rates does to the economic value of the bank. *Economic value* is defined as the net present value of the assets less the net present value of the liabilities, and the net present value of the off balance sheet items. In concept, it is the same as the market value approach noted above. The difference is that because the OCC approach is designed to collect data in a uniform fashion, it has specified many of the behavioral assumptions about retail deposits and mortgages. Each balance sheet category is assigned risk factors on the basis of interest rates moving up and down 2 percent. Mortgages and mortgage products receive special treatment designed to capture their option features.

CRITERIA FOR CHOOSING AN APPROACH

Asset/liability models serve a number of purposes besides identifying interest rate exposure. From an interest rate exposure point of view, a model should

1. clearly define the current macro sensitivity of your bank to changes in rates
2. identify basis risk
3. identify option risk
4. be able to incorporate future plans and events
5. reveal all of the choices for remedying an undesirable exposure
6. be easy to use and understand

The dynamic gap approach satisfies criteria 1, 4, 5, and 6.
The duration gap approach satisfies criteria 1, 5, and 6.
The funds allocation approach satisfies criteria 1, 2, 5, and 6.
The simulation model satisfies criteria 2, 3, 4, and 5.
The market value approach satisfies criteria 1, 2, 3, and 5.

As you can see, the answer rests in using a combination of approaches. The ones chosen will depend on your bank's characteristics.

SOURCES

Darling & Associates, Inc., *Asset/Liability Matrix*, software program, 1984.

Alden L. Toevs and William C. Haney, "Measuring and Managing Interest Rate Risk: A Guide to Asset/Liability Models Used in Banks and Thrifts," in Robert B. Platt, ed., *Controlling Interest Rate Risk*, New York, John Wiley & Sons, 1986, pp. 256-350.

Charles A. Richard III, *Mark-to-Market Accounting and Interest Rate Risk*, presentation to Savings & Community Banker's Annual Convention, November 1992.

Office of the Comptroller of the Currency, "Risk-Based Capital Standards: Interest Rate Risk," *Federal Register*, Vol. 60, No. 48, August 2, 1995, pp. 39490-39572.

CHAPTER 14

Alternatives for Hedging Interest Rate Risk in Banks

The alternatives discussed in previous chapters apply to banks as well as companies. But, as we've seen, banks have a number of unique exposure situations. They can be classed into several types: (1) those resulting from different interest rate indices on assets and the liabilities funding them, (2) those arising in the investment portfolio, (3) those resulting from embedded options, and (4) those being generated by a lack of loan demand. This chapter looks at how bankers can address exposure situations with derivatives. We'll introduce some new derivatives, as well as use ones already discussed.

DIFFERENT INDICES

Let's take another look at the two ways in which rate indices create an exposure, and the possible solutions. The exposures we discussed were created when the rate on the asset and the rate on the liability were different, for example, prime and Libor; and when the rates were the same, but the maturity of the assets was longer than the maturity of the liabilities.

DIFFERENT RATES

Prime loans are funded by Eurodollar deposits, Fed Funds, and bank CDs. As we saw in the previous chapter, the spreads between the asset index and the liability indices widen and narrow. This leads to volatile lending spreads and volatile income. A solution to this exposure is a basis swap, in which the bank pays out prime and receives Libor (or Fed Funds, or T-bill rates). Both legs of the swap are floating rate indices, and the swap fixes the spread between them. To see how the spread is maintained after the basis swap hedge is in place, we'll look at two different rate scenarios in Table 14.1. The spread in the swap is 250 basis points.

Table 14.1 Prime/Libor Swap

Flows	Prime Is 9% Libor Is 6% (%)	Prime Is 11% Libor Is 10% (%)
Loan interest (prime)	9.00	11.00
Funding cost (Libor)	(6.00)	(10.00)
Swap outflow (prime –250)	(6.50)	(8.50)
Swap inflow (Libor)	6.00	10.00
Net lending spread	2.50	2.50

In the scenario on the left, you would pay your counterparty 0.50 percent on the notional amount on settlement day. In the second scenario, your counterparty would pay you 1.50 percent on the notional amount on the settlement day.

The details of a prime/Libor basis swap look like this:

Notional Amount:	$150,000,000
Transaction Date:	September 6, 1996
Effective Date:	September 8, 1996
Maturity Date:	September 8, 1999
Libor Rate Payer Payment Dates:	December 8, March 8, June 8, September 8

Libor Rate Payer:	Swap dealer
Libor Rate Reference:	3-month Libor, Reuters page LIBO
Libor Rate Reset Dates:	March 6, June 6, September 6, December 6
Libor Rate Day Count:	Actual/360
Prime Rate Payer:	Bank
Prime Rate Reference:	Federal Reserve Report H.15
Prime Rate Payment Dates:	December 8, March 8, June 8, September 8
Spread:	Minus 2.50%
Prime Rate Day Count:	Actual/360
Method of Averaging:	Weighted
Business Day Convention:	Modified following business day

The portion of the prime loan portfolio funded by Fed Funds can be hedged by a prime/Fed Funds basis swap. The principles are the same as the prime/Libor basis swap. The indices are two floating rates with a fixed spread established between them.

Other alternatives for hedging the prime loan portfolio depend on your taking a view on the direction of rates. Because there are many alternatives to choose from, especially with two interest rates that can be hedged, you need a way to filter through them. One way of making sure that you have considered all the alternatives and their consequences is to go through the following procedure:

- Classify the hedges as to whether or not they fix rates or provide insurance, and whether or not they are symetric or asymetric.
- Consider how the premium on the insurance will be paid. Will it be by paying the full premium or earning premium through another transaction?
- Look at what happens if interest rates go up and if interest rates go down.
- Think about the consequences if just one leg of the exposure were hedged and the other were left unhedged.
- Consider the consequences if both legs are hedged.

Table 14.2 is an example of this process.

Table 14.2 Alternatives for Hedging a Prime Loan Portfolio Funded with Eurodollar Deposits

Hedging Alternatives	Fix a Rate	Insurance	Insurance Payment
Prime	Swap to receive fixed and pay prime	Buy a floor on prime	Sell a cap on prime
Rates up	Narrow	?	Narrow
Rates down	Widen	Widen	Widen
Libor	Swap to pay fixed and receive Libor	Buy a cap on Libor	Sell a floor on Libor
Rates up	Widen	Widen	Widen
Rates down	Narrow	?	Narrow
Both prime and Libor	Equivalent to a prime/Libor basis swap	Buy a floor on prime and and buy a cap on Libor	A collar on prime and a collar on Libor
Rates up	Stable	Widen	?
Rates down	Stable	Widen	?

In the first column, rates are fixed with swaps. In the second column, insurance is provided by a floor on prime and a cap on Libor. In the third column, the floor and cap premiums are offset by selling a cap on prime and selling a floor on Libor. You are concerned with what happens to your lending spread after the hedge. Will it be stable, will it widen, will it narrow, or will you be able to predict what will happen as rates move up or down?

The upper left-hand corner of the table shows what happens if you enter into a swap to receive a fixed rate and pay prime. The Libor rate is unhedged. If interest rates go up, the rate you receive on the loan is fixed, so a rising Libor rate will narrow the margin between the fixed rate and Libor. If interest rates go down, the rate you receive on the loan asset is fixed, so a falling liability rate will widen the margin on the loan portfolio.

The middle of the second column shows what happens if you buy a cap on Libor and leave the prime rate unhedged. If rates go up, earnings on the loan portfolio will rise as prime rises, and Libor is capped. If rates go down, the hedge has no effect, so the effect of the rate movement on your lending spread is not predictable.

The lower right-hand corner of the table shows what happens if you buy a floor on prime and, to reduce the premium, sell a cap. At the same time, you buy a cap on Libor and, to reduce the premium, sell a floor. These are the collars we looked at in Chapter 9. The lending spread is not predictable, but it will fall inside the shaded band shown in Illustration 14.1.

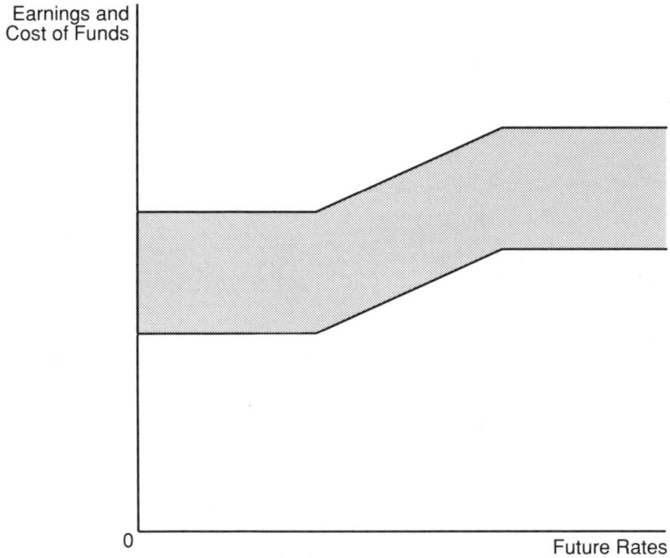

Illustration 14.1 Collars on Prime and Libor

This analysis gives you the framework for a decision. You are able to test your interest rate forecasts against the cost of the hedges and the prospects for your lending spreads.

The derivatives presented for offsetting the insurance premiums are fairly conservative. They were chosen on the principle that you were willing to trade off some benefit of higher rates on prime and lower rates on Libor to reduce the premiums, but not assume additional risk. These collars have the benefit of defining the risks you take.

Other derivatives will reduce the premiums, but they introduce additional risk if you are wrong in your rate forecast. For example, if you think that rates will rise, one alternative is to buy a cap on Libor and offset the premium by selling a floor on prime. If rates do rise, the loan spread widens. If rates fall, however, you could end up losing money. As prime falls below the floor level, you make a net payment on the floor you sold. This causes the net earnings on the loan portfolio to fall faster than Libor falls (see the shaded portion in Illustration 14.2).

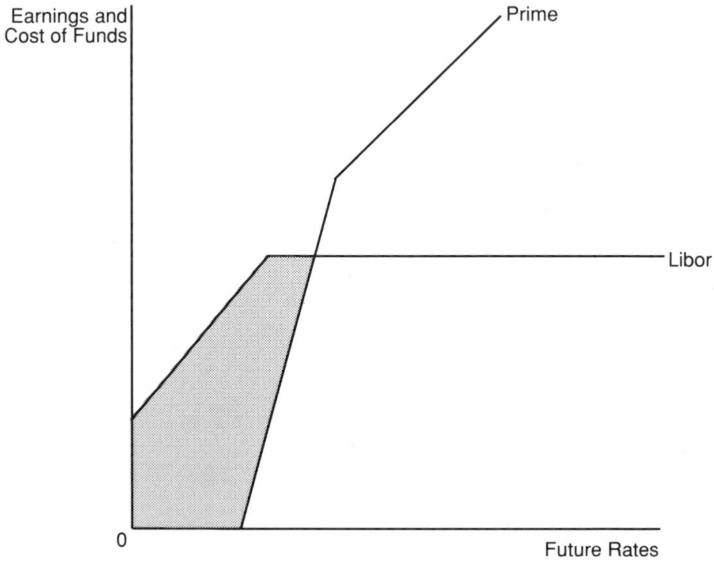

Illustration 14.2 Purchase a Cap on Libor and Sell a Floor on Prime

DIFFERENT MATURITIES

In the previous chapter, we saw that funding six-month loans with one-month deposits can create a high level of volatility in lending spreads. The solutions to this exposure are short term swaps and futures. With short term swaps, the fixed leg may be as short as three months, while the floating leg of the swap is one month. The principles and conventions of these swaps are the same as those where the fixed leg is five years and the floating leg is six months.

The exposure also can be hedged with a strip of futures contracts. In Chapter 7, we talked about the Eurodollar futures contract where the underlying instrument is three-month Eurodollar deposits. In a Libor futures contract, the underlying instrument is one-month Eurodollar deposits. The discussion of the pros and cons of using Eurodollar futures contracts also applies to Libor contracts. However, because the contracts are on one-month deposits rather than three-month deposits, the timing risks are moderated considerably.

INVESTMENT PORTFOLIO

The portion of the investment portfolio classified as held-to-maturity is difficult to adjust to changing market conditions. In a period of rising rates, a bank may find that the duration of its bond portfolio is longer than desired. Rather than buying shorter dated securities to reduce the duration of the portfolio, it can use a swap to accomplish the same results. To see how this works, let's first look at the duration of a swap and how it affects the duration of a bond portfolio.

The duration of a swap is equal to the duration of the fixed rate leg minus the duration of the floating rate leg. The duration of the fixed leg of a five-year swap with a 6 percent coupon is the same as the duration of a five-year note with a 6 percent coupon. The calculation of the duration of a five-year, 6 percent swap with a floating leg tied to six-month Libor is:

Fixed leg:	4.48 years
Floating leg:	(0.50) years
Duration of swap:	3.98 years

When you add shorter term bonds to a portfolio, the resulting portfolio duration is the average of the longer bonds and the shorter bonds. Adding a swap where you pay the fixed rate, however, results in a direct reduction of the portfolio's duration. Let's look at the case of a single 10-year 6 percent bond with a duration of 7.83 years. If you buy a 5-year 6 percent bond in the same amount, the duration of the portfolio is now 6.16 years—the average of 7.83

and 4.48 years. If you enter into a 5-year swap to pay a fixed rate of 6 percent with a notional amount equal to the 10-year bond, the duration of the portfolio is now 3.85 years—7.83 years minus 3.98 years. The swap is a more effective way to reduce the duration of the portfolio and its sensitivity to rising rates.

The swap also can be used to extend the duration and interest rate sensitivity of a portfolio. To extend duration, you would enter into a swap where you receive the fixed rate and pay the floating rate.

EMBEDDED OPTIONS

As we saw in the previous chapter, the problem with embedded options is that customers pay off high-rate mortgages when rates go down and refinance at lower rates. The bank is usually not able to shift the rate down on its liabilities at the same pace. The result is that the bank's income falls.

DEFINING THE EXPOSURE

To structure a hedge for the mortgage portfolio, the first step is to divide the portfolio into different segments. Mortgage portfolios are not homogeneous. Mortgages carry different rates and are often tied to different interest rate indices. Prepayment will depend on the current rate structure of each bank's portfolio, the behavior of the customer base, and the mortgage products the competition is offering. Historical experience will help you model the prepayment characteristics of each segment of the portfolio. Prepayment is generally triggered as market interest rates fall below the rate prevailing in each segment of the mortgage portfolio. For hedging, it makes sense to structure a hedge for each rate and index segment of the portfolio. As a note of caution, even after the portfolio is modeled and segmented, you should not expect the hedges to be perfect, since customer behavior is not predictable. It is, however, worthwhile to implement a hedging program to protect income. An imperfect hedge that does not generate additional risk is better than none.

HEDGING ALTERNATIVES FOR THE MORTGAGE PORTFOLIO

Three alternatives that have been used to hedge the exposure of mortgage portfolios are floors, digital floors, and index accreting swaps. An *index accreting swap* is one in which the notional amount of the swap increases as a specified interest rate index goes down. The accretion schedule is specified in the terms of the transaction. An accretion schedule may look like this:

Change in the Index	Accretion of Notional Amount
– 1%	110%
– 2%	125%
– 3%	140%

Index accreting swaps generally start out at a lower rate than a traditional swap, in order to pay for the options embedded in them. These options effectively layer-in additional swaps as rates decline.

To hedge a mortgage portfolio segment, you would either buy a floor, buy a digital floor, or receive a fixed rate on the index accreting swap. The hedging program will be more efficient if some derivatives are arranged to start in the future rather than today. This would be the case in the situation where mortgage rates are at 7 percent, you have a mortgage portfolio segment priced at 5 percent, and rates are not expected to decline precipitously.

Illustration 14.3 shows how the various alternatives behave with changes in future rates. All of the alternatives are structured to protect at the same rate level, denoted as **R.** When the floor level is reached, you will be compensated for the difference between the index rate and market rates, so a given rate level will be protected. In protecting the income of a mortgage portfolio, a floor protects the income level for a given notional amount but does not compensate you if you lose mortage balances in the refinancing process.

The digital floor can be structured to provide additional payoff when the floor level is reached. Thereafter the return from the digital floor hedge declines with market rates. Once rates fall to a given level, a digital floor generates additional income. If mortgage payoffs are triggered at certain rate levels, you will receive a one-time compensation for the loss of income.

The index accreting swap returns a lower rate than a traditional swap before it begins to accrete, but then effectively increases the return to the original amount of the swap as the accretion begins. The index accreting swap mirrors most closely the rate and balance problems when mortgages are refinanced. It effectively adds balances back at the same rate at which they were lost. To some extent, this is offset by the low return when rates remain above the level at which accretion begins.

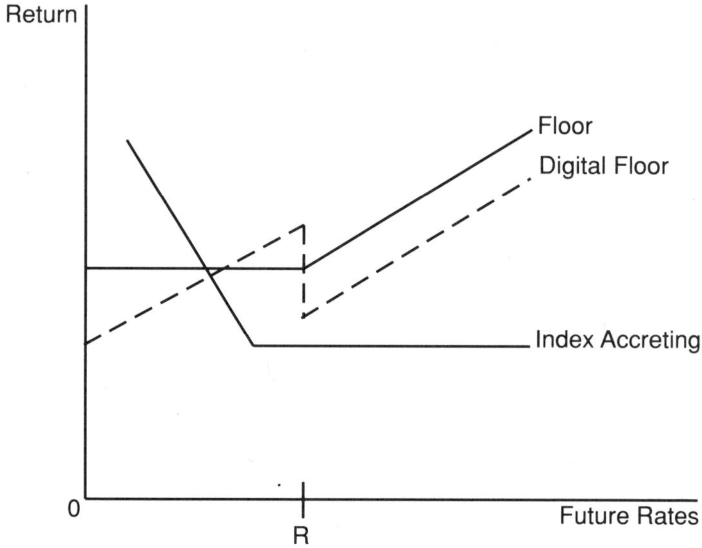

Illustration 14.3 Alternatives for Hedging a Mortgage Portfolio

LACK OF LOAN DEMAND

Banks are reluctant to chase away depositors when loan demand is slack because deposits are the entree for selling other bank services. But depositing these excess funds in the Fed Funds market results in thinner margins. Buying securities creates interest rate and liquidity risks, especially if the money is needed prior to the maturity of the securities. To address this situation, banks have employed swaps to receive a fixed rate, index amortizing swaps, and structure notes.

SWAPS

A swap to receive a fixed rate moves you out the yield curve and generates a higher return. At the same time, cash is available if loan demand picks up unexpectedly. The likelihood of this swap producing undesirable results is low, since you do not have to undo the swap when loan demand picks up.

When loan demand is slack, the earnings and costs are:

Earnings on short term deposit of cash	Libor
Pay the floating rate on the swap	(Libor)
Receive the fixed rate on the swap	Treasury plus swap spread
Net return	Treasury plus swap spread

When loan demand picks up, the earnings and costs are:

Earnings on the loan	Libor, or prime plus loan spread
Pay the floating rate on the swap	(Libor)
Receive the fixed rate on the swap	Treasury plus swap spread
Net return	Treasury plus loan spread plus swap spread

You will incur an opportunity cost if short term rates rise above the fixed rate on the swap. This likelihood can be mitigated by keeping the maturity of the swap on the short side.

INDEX AMORTIZING SWAP

The attraction of an index amortizing swap is that it offers the receiver an above-market fixed rate. The additional earnings can be from 50 to 100 basis points. In an *index amortizing swap*, the notional amount of the swap amortizes as short term rates decline. A typical structure is:

Notional amount:	$100,000,000—when the notional amount amortizes to 15 percent of the notional amount the swap terminates
Stated Maturity:	3 years
Lock out period (notional amount does not change):	1 year
Amortization frequency:	Quarterly
Rate reset frequency:	Quarterly
Fixed rate:	5.75%
Floating rate:	4%
Amortization:	On each quarterly reset following the lockout period, the notional amount of the swap amortizes based on the change in rates *from* the current three-month Libor:

Change in Libor	Amortization
+ 4%	10%
+ 3	15
+ 2	25
+ 1	50
0	60
– 1	75
– 2 or more	100

The index amortizing swap behaves like a mortgage portfolio since the notional amount of the swap declines as rates fall. With the swap, however, the amount falls on a predictable schedule. Many banks have used this swap to generate incremental return when loan demand is low and interest rates are expected to fall.

To see the attraction and risks of this swap, compare the fixed rate on the index amortizing swap with comparable fixed rates on a standard one-year swap (lock out period) and a standard three-year swap (final maturity).

One-year standard swap:	5.00%
Three-year standard swap:	6.50%
Index amortizing swap:	5.75%

The index amortizing swap is attractive if rates are stable or are expected to fall. You will earn a premium above shorter term market rates. If rates rise, however, the swap does not amortize very rapidly, and you earn less than you could have from a standard swap. These swaps were very attractive to banks from 1991 through 1993 when rates were falling. They were very unattractive in 1994 when short term interest rates rose rapidly. A number of well-known financial institutions took write-offs to reflect the decline in the value of these instruments.

Index amortizing swaps and index accreting swaps are structured by combining a standard swap with swaptions. With the index amortizing swap, you sell options to the derivatives dealer to cancel portions of the swap as rates fall. With the index accreting swap, you buy options to enter into swaps in additional amounts as rates fall. The unique part of both structures is that the rates that trigger the options are short term interest rates, not longer term fixed rates.[1]

STRUCTURED NOTES

Banks and other investors buy structured notes because they can be customized to fit their unique requirements and because they allow banks to obtain higher than market yields if certain interest rate scenarios occur. Structured notes are combinations of garden variety securities and derivatives. Government agencies, like Federal Home Loan Bank and Federal Farm Credit Banks, are the largest issuers of structured notes. Over $150 billion were issued in 1993 and 1994. These notes led Orange County, California, other local government entities, and mutual funds into trouble in 1994 and 1995. The reason for considering them here is that many banks and their customers have bought them. They are valuable tools when understood and used appropriately. We will look at a couple of structures, examine the components, and suggest how they should be evaluated. This will not be a full treatment of the subject. Anyone who is serious about investing in structured securities should read Peng and Dattatreya's recent book, *The Structured Note Market*.[2]

Inverse Floating Rate Note

One of the most common structures is the inverse floating rate note. It is attractive to people who think rates will fall. The coupon on the note is usually expressed as a fixed rate minus Libor, for example, 14 percent – Libor. The inverse floater is made up of a standard floating rate note that pays Libor and two interest rate swaps. The construction of the note is:

Receive on *two* 7% interest rate swaps:	14%
Pay on *two* interest rate swaps:	(2 × Libor)
Receive on the floating rate note:	Libor
Net return:	14% – Libor

The investor is doing two things: (1) investing funds to buy a floating rate note and (2) borrowing at Libor to receive the stream of income on two fixed rate notes (the swaps). As with any leveraged investment, the results are very attractive when the market goes in the right direction. The results are ugly when the market goes the other way. Illustration 14.4 depicts the returns from possible future rates. At inception, the yield on the inverse floating rate note is superior to a fixed rate note and to a standard floating rate note. When rates fall, the yield becomes particularly attractive. Rates do not have to rise very much, however, before the inverse floater begins to under perform both the fixed rate note and the standard floating rate note. This is the effect of the leverage embedded in the inverse floater. We're looking at an inverse floater with two swaps structured into it; notes have been issued with as many as 10 swaps embedded. The risk and return characteristics are even more dramatic.

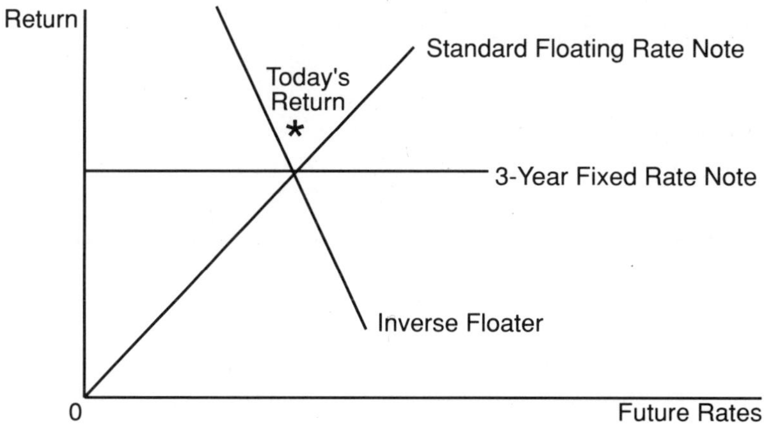

Illustration 14.4 Inverse Floating Rate Note

CALLABLE STEP-UP NOTE

The appeal of the callable step-up note is similar to the inverse floating rate note. The investor is offered a rate for the non-call period that is higher than could otherwise be obtained for the same maturity. An example is:

Notional Amount:	$25,000,000
Maturity:	3 years
Coupon for years 1 and 2:	7%
Coupon for year 3:	8.3%
Call feature:	Callable by the issuer at par after 2 years

The investor is doing two things: (1) investing in a standard three-year note and (2) selling the issuer the option to cancel the note after two years—a swaption. (This is the same transaction we looked at in Chapter 11 from the company's perspective. The only difference is the step-up rate feature.) The issuer turns around and sells the same option in the derivatives market at a higher premium. This enables the issuer to pay a premium rate for the first two years and the step-up rate in the third year. But, the issuer does not pass through as much as it earns. If it did, it would not have much of an incentive to issue a callable note and enter into a derivatives transaction.

There is more than one way to evaluate the value of a callable step-up note. The first way is to value each component. You determine the rate at which the company issues standard three-year debt and determine the premium in the derivatives market for an option to cancel a three-year swap two years from now. The sum of the note rate and the premium is the value of the note. The second way is to calculate the internal rate of return on a standard three-year note and on the callable step-up note, assuming it goes to maturity. A third way is to calculate the forward rate for the step-up period and compare that to the rate being offered for the period. It is not a bad idea to check value by using all three methods; you obtain a fuller insight into your own rate assumptions.

The risk of buying a callable step-up note is that it is not called. This happens when rates rise above the stepped-up rate in the third year. As a result, you earn less than you could have with a standard investment.

Constant Maturity Note

A constant maturity treasury (CMT) note offers attractive yields and avoids the need to take an outright view on interest rates. Instead, you take a view on how short rates will move relative to long rates along the yield curve. A sample structure is:

Notional amount:	$50,000,000
Maturity:	3 years
Coupon:	(10 year CMT – 2 year CMT) + 3.50
Rate reset period:	Semiannual

The components of this note are a standard three-year note and a *CMT swap*. A CMT swap is a basis swap like those we looked at earlier in this chapter. Instead of using short term indices like Libor and Fed Funds, the CMT swap uses longer term indices, like Treasury note and Treasury bond yields. CMT rates are published in the Federal Reserve *Statistical Report* H. 15(519). The following scenarios illustrate the structure:

Rate on the note:	5.50%
Receive 10-year CMT – 2.00%:	5.00%
Pay 2-year CMT:	(5.00%)
Return for the first six months:	5.50%

You get the same answer by expressing the return in the same fashion as the coupon is expressed:

(10-year CMT – 2 year CMT) + 3.50%
7% – 5% + 3.50% = 5.50%

This note yields excellent returns when the yield curve becomes steeper, but does poorly when short term rates rise more rapidly than long term rates, as happened in 1994. Evaluating how structured notes tied to more than one index will perform requires different tools than those we used to look at inverse floaters and callable step-up notes.

Peng and Dattatreya use duration to evaluate the sensitivity of structured notes to changes in interest rates. Recall that for a fixed rate note, the coupon rate and prevailing market rates are used to calculate duration. The coupon determines the cash flows of the note, and prevailing market rates are used to discount these cash flows. With structured notes, however, changes in market interest rates affect both the return on the note and the discount rate. Therefore, to determine the sensitivity of a structured note to changes in rates, duration is calculated for all of the return components of the note and the discount rate, and then combined to get net duration.

Before You Buy

This section on structured notes has provided only an outline of the ways to determine the value of notes and their sensitivity to changes in interest rates. Because notes are not as transparent as swaps and caps, and their outcome depends on a particular view of interest rates, investors need to know more and know it better. If you cannot figure out how to break the note into its component parts, value them, and assess the exposure to interest rate movements, ask the person who is selling them to you. And if you still do not understand, don't buy.

NOTES

1. Sources of information on index swaps are Robert W. Kopprasch, "Using Swaps in the Fixed-Income Portfolio," in Keith C. Brown, ed., *Derivative Strategies for Managing Portfolio Risk,* Charlottesville, Virginia, Association for Investment Management and Research, 1993, pp. 27-30; and The Globecon Group, Ltd., *The Derivatives Engineering Workbook,* Chicago, Irwin Professional Publishing, 1995, pp. 214-223.

2. Scott Y. Peng and Ravi E. Dattatreya, *The Structured Note Market*, Chicago, Probus Publishing Company, 1995. Also see Galen Burghardt and Bill Hoskins, "Hedging Extension & Compression Risk in Callable Agency Notes," *Research Note*, Dean Witter Institutional Futures, March 24, 1995.

CHAPTER 15

Walking Through a Transaction

This chapter pulls together the strands of the book and looks at two cases, one with a company and one with a bank. We'll start from the time the exposure is created and go until the accounting entries are made. We'll assume that the important work of establishing a hedging policy and setting up the appropriate infrastructure to control and monitor transactions has been done.

A COMPANY

Your company has $250 million in floating rate debt, $100 million in fixed rate debt, and $150 million in equity. Net income over the last three years has averaged $15 million. The company is leveraged and income generation is weak. You have convinced management to take a look at hedging a portion of the floating rate debt to reduce the exposure. You collect a number of interest rate forecasts, including the market's forecast as embodied in the forward curve, to demonstrate the impact of rate changes on the company. Illustration 15.1 shows the change in interest expense for four different forecasts over 12 quarters.

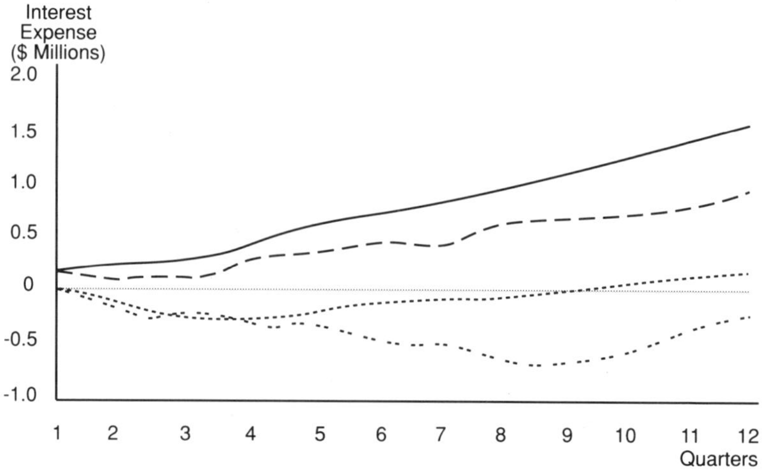

Illustration 15.1 Change in Interest Expense—Four Forecasts

In the best case, the company picks up a benefit of about $500,000 a quarter. In the worst case, its interest expense is an additional $1,600,000 a quarter, compared to net income of $3,750,000 a quarter. Because of the severe risk of rising rates and other analyses you present, you convince management that the company should hedge its interest rate exposure.

The next step is to select derivatives dealers as potential counterparties. If you do not know any dealers, your local bank can guide you and provide introductions. You obtain the ISDA Master Agreement, *User's Guide* and *Definitions,* so that you and your legal counsel understand the agreement that binds parties in derivatives transactions. Because entering into a derivatives transaction involves credit considerations, you start the process of having your company's credit approved and, within your company, of having the credit of the potential counterparties approved.

Now the process of examining the various alternatives for hedging your floating rate debt begins. Derivatives dealers present different alternatives for hedging the exposure. You evaluate the dealers on their understanding of the risks you face and your objectives, how well tailored the proposed hedge alternatives are to your exposure, the dealer's thoroughness in comparing alternatives and illustrating their performance under different rate scenarios, and the dealer's alertness to the tax and accounting implications of the transactions. Then you begin to negotiate Master Agreements with your prospective counterparties. You narrow down the alternatives to swaps, caps, collars, and corridors and price them for a three-year maturity.

Swap	6.00%
Cap	
6% strike	2.05% premium
7% strike	1.15% premium
Collar	1.60% premium
Cost: Buy 6% cap	2.05% premium
Earn: Sell 4.75% floor	0.45% premium
Corridor	1.00% premium
Cost: Buy 6% cap	2.05% premium
Earn: Sell 7% cap	1.05% premium

After looking at the cost of the corridor compared to the collar, you decide that, in these circumstances, the corridor is too risky and not appropriate for the company. The company would lose protection when rates went above 7 percent, just when it was most needed. You analyze the three remaining alternatives under four different rate scenarios and decide to execute three-year swaps for up to $150 million.

Your next step is to present the hedging program to the board and obtain a corporate resolution allowing the company to enter into swaps. You sign the Master Agreements with at least *three* derivatives dealers, to ensure that when it comes time to execute the transactions, you have a choice.

Rates on your floating rate loans reset at three different times, so you decide to break up the hedge program into three pieces of $50 million each. One of the virtues of OTC derivatives is the ability to tailor hedges precisely, so you specify that the reset dates on the swaps match the reset dates on the underlying exposure. Prior to executing a transaction, you send a fax to the dealers with the details, including amount, dates, floating rate index, day count conventions—all of the details in the confirmation. Written details are especially important when you want the hedge to match the exposure tightly. After sending the fax, you call one or two of the dealers to get a feel for what the price should be and how they are pricing. You want to have an idea of what the number is going to look like when you call to execute.

When it's time to execute a transaction, assemble three people with three phones in a room and call three different dealers at the same time. Ask for their quote on your transaction. If the calls and quotes are not simultaneous, you have no guarantee that the three rates are comparable, because the market may have moved. You must decide quickly on which quote to accept.

Confirmation from the dealer should arrive within 24 hours of the trade. Before sending them to operations and accounting, carefully check the confirmation to ensure that all of the details are correct.

Although the accounting profession has not issued a definitive statement on accounting for derivative transactions, there is consensus on some basic principles. If the derivative is being used to hedge an asset or liability, and the terms of the derivative correspond to the terms of the asset or liability being hedged, then the derivative can be integrated with the underlying instrument. For example, if you make a payment on a swap that hedges a floating rate loan, it would be accounted for as an addition to interest expense. If you receive a payment, it would be accounted for as a reduction of interest expense. But, if the derivative is not being used to hedge an asset or liability, currently on the books or anticipated, then it is marked to market periodically, and the change in value from one period to the next is recorded as income.

The basic accounting entries for your loans and the swaps are:

Instrument	**Debit**	**Credit**
Loan	Interest expenses (Libor plus loan spread)	Interest payable
Swap	Interest expense (fixed leg)	Interest expense (floating leg, Libor) Swap payable (difference between the fixed rate payment and the floating rate payment. It can be either a credit or debit depending on whether you are a net payer or receiver on the swap)

Each quarter, you disclose derivative transactions in the footnotes to your financial statements.[1] The details include:

- the notional amount
- the tenor
- the fixed rate
- the index
- the credit risk amount
- the fair value (current market value)
- the effect of a 1-percent rate change on the fair value

The credit risk amount may be larger than the fair value, if your swaps have both positive and negative current values. In the current situation, the credit risk amount and the fair value are the same since the swaps were done in the same sense on the same day. The disclosure for your company would look like the following:

> *Summary of Accounting Policies (in Part)*
> The company enters into interest rate swap and cap agreements in the management of interest rate exposure. The differential to be paid or received is normally accrued periodically as interest rates change and is recognized over the life of the agreements.
>
> *Commitments and Contingencies (in Part)*
> The company has entered into interest rate swap agreements to reduce the impact of changes in interest rates on its floating rate, long term debt. At March 31, 19XX, the company has three interest rate swaps with commercial and investment banks, having a total notional amount of $150 million. In each swap, the company pays a fixed rate and receives a rate indexed to six-month Libor. These agreements effectively change the company's interest rate exposure on its $50 million syndicated bank loan due in 19XX to 7.00 percent and on its $100 million syndicated bank loan due in 20XX to 7.52 percent. The interest rate swap agreements mature in May 19XX, July 19XX, and September 20XX. The company is exposed to a credit loss in the amount of the fair value of the swaps in the event of nonperformance by its counterparties to the swap agreements. At March 31, 19XX, this amounts to $358,000. A 1-percent shift in interest rates will affect the fair value by $3,995,000. The company does not anticipate nonperformance by the counterparties.

A BANK

Your bank raises most of its funds by issuing three- and six-month certificates of deposit in the region. The consensus of the asset/liability committee is that rates are trending upward. Your interest rate sensitivity model indicates that if rates go up more than 2 percent from current levels, the bank's margins will be squeezed. After examining the alternatives, you decide to buy a cap that is 2 percent above current rate levels.

What index should you use on the cap? You know that Libor is the most common index for caps, but this does not correspond to your funding. Your CD rates are set with an eye to the Fed Funds rate, Treasury bill rates, and what the competition is paying. After looking at how well the CD rates track various indices, you decide that it makes sense to buy a cap where the index is the three-month Treasury bill rate. Your execution of the cap transaction with derivatives dealers will parallel the procedure followed by the company.

Financial institutions that file the FFIEC Reports (Call Reports) use Schedule RC-L, items 14 through 17, to record the notional amount and fair values of their interest rate contracts.

The accounting conditions under which the payments on a cap and other options, like products, can be integrated with the underlying instrument are somewhat more restrictive than for swaps. You have to demonstrate a high correlation between the hedge and the exposure—in this instance, your CD rates and Treasury bill rates. You have to continue to monitor this correlation. If the correlation cannot be demonstrated, the cap is marked to market periodically, and the difference from one period to the next flows to the income statement. Assuming the correlation is good, the premium is amortized over the period of the option or over the period hedged by the option. And, if you receive a payment from the bank because floating rates go above the cap rate, the payment is treated as a reduction of interest expense.

These few paragraphs on accounting have only highlighted the issues you should think about. It is recommended that you talk to your accountant about the accounting and the tax implications of the transactions you intend to enter into—before you do it.

SOURCES

Financial Accounting Standards Board, *Statement of Financial Accounting Standards No. 105, Disclosure of Information about Financial Instruments with Off-Balance-Sheet Risk and Financial Instruments with Concentrations of Credit Risk,* Financial Accounting Series, March 1990.

Financial Accounting Standards Board, *Statement of Financial Accounting Standards No. 107, Disclosures about Fair Value of Financial Instruments,* Financial Accounting Series, December 1991.

Financial Accounting Standards Board, *Statement of Financial Accounting Standards, No. 119, Disclosure about Derivative Financial Instruments and Fair Value of Financial Instruments,* Financial Accounting Series, October 1994.

Descriptions of Derivative Products

accreting cap, floor, swap: These transactions are used to hedge construction loans and growing working capital requirements. The notional amount of the cap, floor, or swap increases on a scheduled basis over the life of the transaction. For example, in the first year, your company hedges $50 million; in the second year, $65 million; in the third year, $75 million. These amounts are specified when you enter into the transaction. The principal risk is that the underlying exposure becomes mismatched with the hedge, and you end up either underhedged or overhedged for a period of time; for example, when bad weather delays construction and the drawdown of the construction loan. Other names are *construction loan*, and *staged drawdown*, *caps, floors*, or *swaps*.

American swaption: See *swaption*.

amortizing cap, floor, swap: These transactions are used to hedge loans where the principal declines on a scheduled basis and to hedge investments that pay out principal over time. The notional amount of the cap, floor, or swap decreases on a scheduled basis over the life of the transaction. For example, in the first year, your company hedges $50 million; in the second year, $25 million; in the third year, $10 million. These amounts are specified when you enter into the transaction. The principal risk in these transactions is that the underlying exposure becomes mismatched with the hedge.You end up either underhedged or overhedged when the company is able to pay off its loan earlier than it anticipated.

arrears option swap: This derivative allows a company to pay a fixed rate and receive a floating rate set either up front or in arrears. The company will receive the more favorable rate. For example, if the rate is 6 percent on the first floating rate reset day and 6.50 percent on the arrears reset day, you will receive 6.50 percent. To pay for this option, you pay a higher fixed rate than in a standard swap. If floating rates increase over the term of the swap, you are better off. If floating rates are fairly constant over the term of the swap, you end up paying a higher rate than you otherwise would have.

Companies also use this swap to hedge short term investments. Most often investors choose to receive a higher fixed rate and give their counterparty the option of choosing the first or arrears floating rate. If short term rates are stable or decline, you benefit; if they rise, your net return from the swap is less. An arrears option swap is also called a *chooser swap*. See *in-arrears swap*.

Asian cap, floor: See *average rate cap, floor*.

asset swap: This allows you to convert the fixed payment stream from a bond into a floating rate payment stream without any slippage between the terms of the swap and the bond. The coupon on the swap, the payment dates, the day count convention, and all other terms of the agreement are matched to a bond held by you, the investor. There is no inherent risk in the instrument. You only have the risk that you could have earned more from the fixed rate on the bond than by swapping it into a floating rate. An asset swap also can be used to convert a floating rate note into a fixed rate earnings stream by matching the terms of the note with the terms of the floating leg of the swap.

average rate cap, floor: Average rate caps are used when a company's loans are priced the same way. This applies to frequent issuers of commercial paper and companies borrowing at prime. On each settlement day, the strike rate on the cap or floor is compared to the average of the indexed rate over a period. For example, a 10 percent cap on prime is compared to the daily average of prime rates during the last 90 days. An average rate cap or floor will have a lower premium than a cap or floor when the strike rate is compared to the index rate on one day.

You might also use an average rate cap if you are borrowing on the basis of three-month Libor. Rather than settle four times a year, the four rates would be averaged, and then compared to the cap rate. This effectively caps overall interest expense, and the premium is lower than for a standard cap. Average caps and floors are also called *Asian caps* and *floors*.

back-set swap: See *in-arrears swap*.

barrier cap, floor: A barrier cap or floor behaves like a standard cap or floor except that its existence depends on Libor, or any index you choose, crossing a threshold level or barrier. There are two kinds of barrier caps and floors: knock-out and knock-in. With a knock-out cap or floor, protection *ceases to exist* if Libor crosses the barrier. With a knock-in cap or floor, protection *exists only* if Libor crosses the barrier. A one-time barrier will knock out or knock in protection for one period only. A sticky barrier will knock out or knock in protection for the remaining term of the transaction. The barrier rate can be either above or below the cap or floor rate, depending on the company's interest rate views. One of the principal attractions of barrier caps and floors is that their premiums are less than regular caps and floors because there is a chance they may not exist.

For example: you want to protect yourself against rates going above 9 percent. Therefore, you buy a three-year, knock-out, sticky barrier cap on Libor at 9 percent. You set the barrier at 6 percent because you feel that if rates ever reach that level during the three-year period, the likelihood of going back up to 9 percent is small. Clearly your risk is that your expectations are confounded—Libor goes to 5.75 percent, protection of the cap ceases, then 18 months later Libor is 9.50 percent. At the point where the cap is knocked out, you should take a new look at its hedging strategy. (See *cap, floor*.)

barrier swaptions: A barrier swaption behaves like a regular swaption, except that its existence depends on the swap coupon crossing a threshold level or barrier. There are two kinds of barrier swaptions: knock-out and knock-in. With a knock-out swaption, protection ceases to exist if the swap rate crosses the barrier. With a knock-in swaption, the protection exists only if the swap rate crosses the barrier. The swap rate used as a reference rate for the barrier usually matches the underlying swap in the swaption. The barrier rate can be either above or below the swaption rate, depending on your interest rate views. With a knock-in swaption, a barrier below the current rate will boost the fixed coupon rate on the swap, while a barrier above the current rate will lower the fixed coupon. One of the principal attractions of barrier swaptions is that their premiums are less than regular swaptions because there is a chance they may not exist.

An example of a barrier swaption: your company wants to hedge against a forthcoming note issue. Ten-year rates one year in the future are currently 7.50 percent, but you buy a one-year option to pay a fixed rate of 9.00 percent on a ten-year swap and incorporate a knock-in barrier at 8.50 percent. You believe that if rates rise more than 1 percent, they could head much higher. This structure still allows a considerable gap between the point at which the protection of the swaption becomes effective and current rate levels.

The most extensive use of this derivative is by issuers of structured notes with embedded barrier swaptions. The barrier swaption is effectively bought from investors and then sold in the derivatives market at a profit, which is then used to lower the issuer's funding cost.

basis swap: Basis swaps are used by banks to hedge the mismatch between the index of their assets and the index of their liabilities, and by swap dealers to create structures for companies to hedge indices other than Libor. With a basis swap, the parties pay a floating rate of interest, and each is tied to a different index. In most basis swaps, the Libor rate is set at the beginning of the period; the other index is calculated as an average of daily or weekly rates over the period. For example, at the beginning of a 90-day period Libor is set at 5.875 percent; 90 days later the daily average of the commercial paper rate is calculated as 5.82 percent. The basis swap sets a spread between the two indices for the life of the transaction. For example, one party pays Libor, the other party pays the commercial paper rate, and the spread is five basis points.

The swap market trades in fixed rates versus Libor. To create a fixed rate versus commercial paper rate swap for a customer, the dealer puts together a fixed rate versus Libor swap with a commercial paper/Libor basis swap.

The following seven paragraphs describe different types of basis swaps, including: COFI/Libor, commercial paper/Libor, Fed Funds/Libor, JJKenny/Libor, prime/Libor, PSA/Libor, and T-bill/ Libor.

COFI/Libor: This basis swap is used primarily by financial institutions to hedge the risk between the returns on their mortgage portfolios and Libor funding. COFI is the acronym for Eleventh District Costs of Funds Index. This index, a composite of long and short term rates, mirrors the funding structure of savings and loans in the Western U.S. The rate for a given reset day is the monthly average for the previous month. It is generally quoted against one-month Libor.

commercial paper/Libor: For many companies, commercial paper is the only floating rate debt they have. It is less expensive than bank loans. These companies use swaps and caps where commercial paper is the floating rate index. The commercial paper rate index is the daily average of the 30-day commercial paper rates for nonfinancial companies rated A-1/P-1 published in the Federal Reserve *Statistical Report* H.15. It is generally quoted against three-month Libor. The risk for companies using the commercial paper as a hedge index is that the rates on *their* commercial paper do not track the index published by the Federal Reserve. This can happen because their commercial paper is not rated the same as the paper used in the index, or the company experiences a sudden rise or fall in its financial health.

Fed Funds/Libor: This basis swap is generally used by banks to hedge an asset/liability mismatch. The Fed Funds rate index is the daily average rate published in the Federal Reserve *Statistical Report* H.15. It is generally quoted against one-month Libor.

JJKenny/Libor: Kenny swaps are used by banks to hedge holdings of tax exempt bonds in their portfolios. Fixed rate swaps with Kenny as the floating index are used by municipalities to hedge their floating and fixed rate debt. The Kenny index reflects rates on short term, floating rate, tax-exempt municipal paper. Compiled by surveying municipal paper dealers, the index is published weekly by J.J.Kenny Service. The weekly average Kenny rate is generally quoted against three-month Libor. The risk to municipalities who hedge floating rate debt with these derivatives is that their rates may vary from the composite index, either because they lie on the fringes of the composite, or their credit rating is in motion. (See *PSA/Libor*.)

prime/Libor: The prime/Libor basis swap is used principally by financial institutions that want to hedge the spread between prime-based assets and Libor-based liabilities. Companies use prime as a floating index in swaps and caps. The prime rate index is the daily average rate published in the Federal Reserve *Statistical Report* H.15. It is generally quoted against three-month Libor.

PSA/Libor: The PSA index is a popular alterntive to JJKenny for hedging holdings of tax-exempt bonds in bank portfolios. Fixed rate swaps with PSA as the floating index are also used by municipalities to hedge their floating and fixed rate debt. The PSA index, published weekly by the Public Securities Association, is the average of a large number of outstanding tax-exempt floating rate issues. The weekly average PSA rate is generally quoted against three-month Libor. The risk to municipalities who hedge floating rate debt with these derivatives is that their rates may vary from the composite index, either because they lie on the fringes of the composite, or their credit rating is in motion. (See *JJKenny/Libor*.)

T-bill/Libor: This basis swap is used by bank asset/liability managers to hedge the risks of T-bill assets and Libor-based funding or Libor loans funded by T-bill-based funding (certificates of deposit and money market accounts). The Treasury bill index is the weekly average rate of the 90-day bill published in the Federal Reserve *Statistical Report* H.15. It is generally quoted against three month Libor.

Bermudan swaption: See *swaption.*

callable swap: See *swaption.*

cap: This agreement puts a ceiling or "cap" on an interest rate. The buyer pays a premium for this protection. In the standard structure, the cap rate is compared to the prevailing market rates every three or six months, to determine if a payment is to be made. For example, a company hedging a floating rate bank loan buys an interest rate cap on $50 million that limits interest expense to 8 percent over the next three years. It pays a premium of $875,000. Every three months, the cap rate is compared to the prevailing three-month Libor rate. The agreement pays the company an amount equal to the difference between market rates and the cap rate times $50 million over three months. The only downside of buying a cap is that when the protection is not needed, the premium might have been saved.

cash flow cap, floor, swap: See *roller coaster cap, floor, swap.*

chooser swap: See *arrears option swap.*

collar: An interest rate collar is a combination of a cap and a floor. As the buyer of a collar, a company purchases a cap to limit the maximum interest rate it will pay and sells a floor to earn a premium to pay for the cap. The effect of the combination is to confine interest rate payments to a range bounded by the strike prices of the cap and floor. An asset manager buys a floor to assure a minimum return on his portfolio and sells a cap to earn a premium to pay for the floor. When the company sells the floor, it gives up the benefit of paying lower interest rates; when the asset manager sells the cap, he or she gives up the benefit of earning higher rates. If the "give ups" are moderate, there is little risk to the company or asset manager. If they become large, they will be disadvantaged relative to their competitors.

constant maturity treasury (CMT) spread cap, floor: CMT caps and floors allow investors to buy or sell options on the shape of the yield curve. CMT caps and floors are more efficient than buying and selling securities of different maturities. These derivatives are seldom used to hedge exposure situations. CMT is a benchmark index based on the yield of a synthetic security of a given maturity as interpolated from the Treasury yield curve. CMT spreads are the difference in basis points between CMTs of two different maturities. If the spread exceeds the cap strike rate, the buyer of the cap receives a payout.

constant maturity treasury (CMT) swap: CMT swaps are used principally for taking a view on the shape of the yield curve. Although they are more efficient than buying and selling securities of the same maturities, they seldom are used to hedge exposure situations. A CMT is a benchmark index based on the yield of a synthetic security of a given maturity as interpolated from the Treasury yield curve. A CMT swap can be structured in three ways:

- One leg is a fixed rate, the other leg floats, a CMT observed every quarter; for example, a fixed rate of 8.54 percent, and a floating rate indexed to a 5-year CMT reset every quarter.
- One leg is a CMT, the other leg is Libor; for example, 3-year CMT versus 6-month Libor reset every six months.
- One leg is a CMT of long maturity and the other leg is a CMT of a short maturity; for example, 10-year CMT versus 2-year CMT reset every three months.

contingent premium cap, floor, swaption: This product is generally viewed as a form of disaster insurance—you need to have interest rate protection, but are unwilling to pay for the costs up front. Instead of paying a premium up front, you pay a premium only if you receive some benefit from the cap, floor, or swaption and only when you receive the benefit. The deferred premium will be significantly higher than the premiums on standard caps, floors, and swaptions. The premium can exceed the payout, in which case you end up as a net payer in the transaction.

construction loan cap, floor, swap: See *accreting cap, floor, swap.*

corridor: The corridor is a combination of two caps, one purchased by a borrowing company at a given rate and the second sold by the company at a higher rate. Generally, the notional amounts of the two caps are the same, but you can have a structure with different amounts. The reason for selling the second cap is to reduce the premium on the first cap. The two-cap structure limits interest costs, unless rates rise through the strike on the upper cap. When that happens, the company's interest costs begin to rise again. The same structure can be executed with swaptions, for the same reasons, and with the same risks.

cumulative cap, floor: Cumulative caps are popular with companies involved in project work because they limit total interest expense. To the extent that rates are below the cap level, they compensate for periods when they are above. For example, when a company is going to borrow $100 million for five years, it does not want its interest expense to exceed $35 million, or 7 percent over the five years. The following schedule illustrates how pay outs are calculated.

Year	Rate (%)	Interest Expense ($)	Cumulative Interest ($)	Pay Out ($)
1	6	6,000,000	6,000,000	0
2	8	8,000,000	4,000,000	0
3	10	10,000,000	24,000,000	0
4	12	12,000,000	36,000,000	1,000,000
5	6	6,000,000	42,000,000	6,000,000

A cumulative cap is appealing for hedging because it is cheaper than a standard cap. It is also possible to add an accreting or amortizing schedule to allow the interest schedule to reflect the borrowing structure of a project. Cumulative caps and floors are also called *Q-caps* and *Q-floors*.

deductible cap, floor: These derivatives protect a company from short-lived interest rate moves. The downside is that the company will be disadvantaged (relative to a standard cap) if a sustained movement in interest rates occurs. Deductible caps and floors are like regular caps and floors, except they pay out only a specified number of times over the life of the transaction. Once the specified number is reached, the cap or floor ceases to exist. The premium for deductible caps and floors is less than for standard caps and floors, since there is a chance that they will cease to exist before the maturity of the transaction. For example, a company buys a cap for four years on three-month Libor. For a reduction in the cap premium, the company agrees that after it has been paid nine times, out of a potential 16, the cap will cease to exist. When the cap goes out of existence, the company must find another way to cover the remaining exposure.

deferred premium cap, floor: This arrangement allows a company to put off paying for a cap or floor. The premium is paid at the end of the transaction instead of at the time the transaction is initiated. The premium will be higher than if it were paid at the beginning, because the dealer is effectively lending the company the premium for a couple of years and is taking the risk that the company will pay when due. It is different than a contingent cap or floor where the payment of the premium depends on whether the company received a payment.

deferred start cap, floor, swap: See *forward cap, floor, swap.*

derivatives: Derivatives allow the unbundling of the total risk of an exposure into the risk's component parts. They make it easier to transfer the components of risk to people who are better able and willing to bear them. A derivative is an instrument whose value or payout is tied to another rate, price, or index. For example, a swap is a derivative because its value changes with changes in Treasury note rates and its payout changes with changes in Eurodollar rates and Libor.

digital cap, floor: Digital caps and floors are attractive because they are cheaper than standard caps and floors. They are effective for hedging small movements beyond the threshold rate. For large movements, protection is lost. These structures have a fixed, predetermined payoff if the index rate is at or beyond the strike rate. The value of the payout is not affected by the magnitude of the difference. For example, you buy a digital floor at 5 percent to protect against the effect of a fall in rates on your short term investments. You would like to have a payout of 1 percent if interest rates cross the 5-percent threshold. If rates fall to 4.75 percent, you receive a 1-percent payout; if rates fall to 3.50 percent, you still receive a 1-percent payout.

Digital caps can be used in conjunction with standard caps to create a corridor. The digital cap is sold at the same rate level at which the standard cap is purchased. The premium received from selling the digital cap is used to offset the premium paid for the standard cap. It creates a more conservative corridor than selling a standard cap because the risks are fully defined. Digital caps and floors are also called *binary caps* and *floors*. (See *corridor*.)

European swaption: See *swaption*.

floor: This agreement puts a minimum or "floor" on an interest rate. The investor pays a premium for this protection. In the standard structure, the floor rate is compared to the prevailing market rates every three or six months, to determine if a payment is to be made. For example, a floating rate investor buys a 5.50-percent floor on $10 million indexed to six-month Libor for two years and pays a premium of 1.94 percent. Every six months, the cap rate is compared to the prevailing six-month Libor rate. The agreement pays the investor an amount equal to the difference between market rates and the floor rate times $10 million over six months. The only downside of buying a floor is that the protection may not be needed and the premium might have been saved.

forward cap, floor, swap: These are standard caps, floors, or swaps where the terms are agreed upon today, but the transaction does not become effective until a specified date in the future.

forward rate agreement (FRA): This agreement allows a company to fix the rate on future borrowing. The difference between the market rate and this fixed rate is settled in cash on the borrowing date. The settlement amount is discounted by the prevailing market rate. For example: to hedge against the reset on a Eurodollar loan, you buy an FRA at 6.43 percent on three-month Libor for $25 million to settle on September 17. If three-month Libor is above 6.43 percent on September 17, you receive a payment from the bank; if three-month Libor is below 6.43 percent, you pay the bank.

forward spread agreement (FSA): See *swap spread lock.*

in-arrears swap: The attraction of this swap is that when the yield curve is positively sloped, you receive a higher rate than with a standard swap. It is like a standard interest rate swap, except that the floating rate is based on the index rate at the end of the period and applied retroactively to the entire period. When used to hedge floating rate assets, the risks are the same as with a standard swap, where you receive a fixed rate. When an in-arrears swap is used to create floating rate debt from a fixed rate issue, rising rates will impact you more quickly than a standard structure. An in-arrears swap is also called a *back-set swap* or *Libor-in-arrears swap*.

index accreting swap: Index accreting swaps are used to hedge mortgage portfolios against a loss of income when falling rates lead customers to refinance their mortgages. The notional amount of the swap increases on a schedule determined by the movement of an index, Libor, or a constant maturity treasury rate. You have the choice about whether the notional amount increases as rates go up or increases as rates go down. Otherwise the mechanics are the same as a standard swap with fixed and floating legs. The fixed rate on the swap will be lower than on a standard swap, to reflect the premium you pay for the option to enter into additional swaps.

index amortizing swap: These swaps are popular with financial institutions when rates are declining because they pay an above market rate of interest for part of their lives. Often they are used as surrogates for mortgage assets by banks when mortgage originations are low. This swap is seldom used to hedge interest rate exposure situations. With an index amortizing swap, the notional amount of the swap decreases on a schedule determined by the movement of an index, Libor, or a constant maturity Treasury rate. You have a choice about whether the notional amount decreases as rates go up, or decreases as rates go down. Otherwise the mechanics are the same as a standard swap with fixed and floating rate legs. If the swap amortizes as rates go up, the coupon will be below market rates for a swap of the same maturity for the initial period of the swap. If the swap amortizes as rates go down, the coupon will be above market for the initial period of the swap.

knock-in cap, floor, swap, swaption: See *barrier cap, floor, barrier swap, barrier swaption.*

knock-out cap, floor, swap, swaption: See *barrier cap, floor, barrier swap, barrier swaption.*

Libor-in-arrears swap: See *in-arrears swap.*

participating cap: A company buys a participating cap to reduce premium expense, and because it does not believe strongly that rates will rise. A participating cap covers less than 100 percent of the amount of the exposure. It reduces but does not eliminate exposure to an upward rate movement. This structure reduces the premium paid, but clearly leaves you naked on the unhedged exposure.

participating hedge: A structure that combines a swap and a cap. To pay for the cap, the swap coupon rate is set higher than for a standard swap. The attraction is that it allows you to have the benefits of both a swap and a cap.

periodic cap, floor: Mortgage lenders sell caps to their borrowers through adjustable rate mortgages and then buy periodic caps to hedge their exposure. Periodic caps and floors are similar to standard caps and floors, except the cap or floor rate in each period is equal to a predetermined spread above or below the rate from the previous period. Additionally, there may be a lifetime cap or floor. For example, the cap in the first period is 5 percent; in the second period, 6 percent; in the third period, 7 percent. Periodic caps have rate sensitivity characteristics similar to adjustable rate mortgages wherein the change in the mortgage rate from one period to the next may be constrained.

Q-cap, floor: See *cumulative cap, floor.*

ratchet swap: The ratchet swap, a combination of a swap and a periodic cap, is used by mortgage lenders to hedge the risk they have with adjustable rate mortgages (ARMs). Many ARMs carry the provision that the interest rate on the home mortgage can only go up a certain amount each period, regardless of what happens to the index rate. The interest rate on the mortgage continues to go up each period until the foregone interest is collected. With a ratchet swap, a mortgage lender will receive a fixed rate and pay a floating rate that mirrors the behavior of the ARM.

roller coaster cap, floor, swap: A swap in which the notional amount rises and falls over the period of the transaction. It is a combination of an accreting and an amortizing structure. It is also called a *cash-flow cap, floor, swap.*

spread cap, floor: Spread caps and floors are used by banks to hedge the compression of the spread between rate on the asset and rate on the liability. Spread caps and floors are like standard caps and floors, except they are stated in terms of the difference between two rates, not as an absolute rate. For example, you can buy a floor on the difference between prime and Fed Funds, say at 2 percent. If the spread in the market goes below 2 percent, you are compensated for the difference. And your funding margin will benefit if the spread between the two rates rises to 3 percent.

Spread caps and floors also are used for taking a view on a change in the shape of the yield curve, rather than as a hedge. Many spread combinations are possible: a cap on the spread between 12-month Libor and 1-month Libor, a cap on the spread between the two-year swap rate and 6-month Libor, or a floor on the spread between the five-year swap rate and the 3-month Libor.

staged drawdown cap, floor, swap: See *accreting cap, floor, swap.*

step-up and step-down cap, floor, swap: These derivatives are fashioned to address the cash flow characteristics of a project or company. The fixed rate changes over the life of the transaction in a way that is designed from the start. For example, if your company's cash flow is tight in the early years of a project, you would start out with a below-standard fixed rate. When cash flow was more ample, the give-up would be received through a higher fixed rate. The transactions are priced so that the present value of the cash flows are the same as a standard swap, cap, or floor.

swap: Swaps are used by companies and banks to:

- hedge floating rate debt
- convert a fixed rate debt to floating rate debt
- reduce the cost of issuing debt
- hedge the investment portfolio
- match the rate characteristics of their assets with the characteristics of their liabilities

A swap is an agreement, covering a specified time, to exchange periodic payments with a counterparty. The standard interest rate swap is an exchange of fixed interest rate payments for three- or six-month Libor on a notional amount fixed for the life of the transaction. Only net interest payments change hands; there is no exchange of principal. At the beginning of the transaction, the fixed rate is set and the floating rate index is determined. For example, you enter into a five-year swap with a bank to pay a fixed rate of 7.47 percent and receive six-month Libor. When a bank or company uses a swap to hedge exposures, they create certainty. Their risk is that they end up paying more for their liabilities and earning less on their assets than without the hedge. The consequences depend on the financial health of the company and what the competition is doing.

swap spread lock: A swap spread lock is used when swap spreads seem particularly low and you know you will be entering into a swap to hedge floating rate liabilities in the near future. An investor hedging short term assets or a company planning to convert a fixed rate issue to floating rate, however, uses a swap spread lock when the spreads seem to be at their peak. The swap spread lock is an agreement which gives you a guaranteed spread over a specific Treasury rate in a swap agreement starting on a fixed future date or period. The arrangement also can be cash-settled if you decide not to enter into a swap. This agreement allows you to lock in the two components of a swap at different times. It is likely that treasury rates and swap spreads will be attractive at different times, so it makes sense to lock them in that way. The risks in this agreement are the same as in any agreement that fixes rates. If you are a borrower, rates may turn out to be lower than the rate you fixed. If you are an investor, rates may turn out to be higher than the rate you fixed.

swap spread option: A swap spread option is used when swap spreads seem particularly low and you know you will be entering into a swap to hedge floating rate liabilities in the near future. An investor hedging short term assets or a company planning to convert a fixed rate issue to floating rate uses a swap spread option when the spreads seem to be at their peak. This agreement gives you the right, but not the obligation, to enter into a swap starting on a fixed future date or period with a guaranteed spread over a specific Treasury rate. The transaction also can be cash-settled at the expiration of the option if you decide not to enter into a swap. You pay a premium for this option. This agreement allows you to choose to lock in the two components of a swap at different times. It is likely that Treasury rates and swap spreads will be attractive at different times, so it makes sense to lock them in that way. The risks in this agreement are the same as any option. If you are a borrower, rates may turn out to be lower than your option rate. If you are an investor, rates may turn out to be higher than your option rate. And you need not have paid the premium.

swaption: Companies enter into swaptions to hedge against future borrowing, to monetize call options of existing debt, and to cancel or extend swaps when the rate environment changes. A swaption is an option to enter into a swap. At the beginning of the transaction, the terms of the swap and option period are specified. You pay a premium to buy the option. When the option is exercised, you may either enter into the swap or a cash payment will be made if the swap has value. Swaptions are classified as to when they can be exercised—American, European, or Bermudan—and as to your rights as a buyer of the option—to receive the fixed rate, pay the fixed rate, extend the swap, or cancel the swap.

The following six paragraphs describe different types of swaptions, including: American swaption, Bermudan swaption, European swaption, swaption to receive fixed, swaption to pay fixed, and cancelable and extendible swaps.

American swaption: American swaptions are particularly suitable for hedging prospective note issuance by companies, because the hedge preserves the underlying structure of the note. An American swaption can be exercised anytime prior to the expiration date. American swaptions with exercise penalties require a fee when exercised. These fees vary over time, which makes them equivalent to calling a bond above par. These exercise fees reduce the premium and match assets, like bonds callable at premium, more closely than a straight no-penalty swaption.

Bermudan swaption: The Bermudan swaption is often used in the monetization of calls and puts on outstanding debt issues and incorporated in cancelable and extendible swaps. A Bermudan swaption is between an American and a European. Although it can be exercised on more than one date, those dates are specified in advance. Moreover, it has the additional feature of having a fixed final date (option period plus swap tenor). Because of this, the tenor of the underlying swap gets shorter as long as the swaption is not exercised.

European swaption: A European swaption can be exercised only on its expiration date.

swaption to receive fixed: This gives the buyer of the swaption the right to receive the fixed rate on the swap. (Also called a *call swaption.*)

swaption to pay fixed: This gives the buyer of the swaption the right to pay the fixed rate on the swap. This is also called a *put swaption.*

cancelable and extendible swaps: These are the same transactions viewed from different perspectives. A company paying a fixed rate protects itself from a rise in interest rates by extending the swap for a longer period. The buyer of the option has the right to extend the fixed rate on the swap on one or more dates prior to the scheduled maturity. For example, you enter into a three-year swap with the option to extend it to five years. You exercise the option if rates rise.

A company paying a fixed rate protects itself from a fall in interest rates by canceling the swap prior to the time it normally ends. The buyer of the option has the right to cancel the swap on one or more dates prior to the scheduled maturity. For example, you enter into a five-year swap with the option to cancel it after three years. You exercise the option if rates fall.

Treasury lock: Companies use Treasury locks to fix the underlying rate on future note issues. The agreement fixes the price or yield of a specific Treasury issue at some time in the future. At settlement, the difference between the current market and the fixed yield is compared and payment is made. It is similar in structure to a forward rate agreement. However, the underlying instrument is much more specific than three-month Libor. The Treasury issue (coupon and maturity date) is specified—the 6.30

percent maturing 15 September 01. Using a Treasury lock carries two risks. The first is common to any derivative that fixes a future rate—the market may be better when the date arrives. The second is that the company's issuance rate does not track the underlying Treasury rate closely. This occurs when the company's credit standing is in transition.

Treasury options: Companies use Treasury options to hedge the underlying rate on future note issues. This agreement gives you the right to buy or sell a specific Treasury at a specific price. At the end of the option period, the strike price is compared to the current price for the specific issue. When used for hedging, the agreement is usually cash-settled; you do not take delivery or deliver a physical Treasury note. The advantage of Treasury options is that you can take advantage of lower rates at the time you decide to issue a note. The risk is that your company's issuing cost does not mirror the movement in treasuries. This occurs when its credit standing is in motion.

trigger swap: A trigger swap is used when a company wants to lower the fixed rate on a swap it is using to hedge floating rate debt. It works in the following way. You compare Libor this period with Libor last period. If the difference is greater than a specified amount, then the fixed rate goes up by a certain amount. For example, if Libor this period changes more than 60 basis points, the fixed rate goes up 25 basis points. The initial fixed rate for the borrower in this arrangement would be 6.33 percent rather than 6.93 percent on a standard swap.

A trigger swap also can be used by a company that wants to raise the fixed rate it receives on a swap. In this case, if Libor changes more than 60 basis points from one period to the next, the company's fixed rate is reduced by 25 basis points.

The trigger swap works well in those situations where interest rates stay in a tight range over the course of the transaction. If rates become volatile, the company may lose the protection it thought it had.

INDEX

D

E

F